SMALL, LARGE, AND
MEDIAN GROUPS

NEW INTERNATIONAL LIBRARY OF GROUP ANALYSIS

Series Editor: Earl Hopper

Other titles in the Series

SMALL, LARGE, AND MEDIAN GROUPS

The Work of Patrick de Maré

Edited by

Rachel Lenn and Karen Stefano

KARNAC

First published in 2012 by
Karnac Books Ltd
118 Finchley Road, London NW3 5HT

British Library Cataloguing in Publication Data

A C.I.P. for this book is available from the British Library

ISBN 978 1 78049 015 1

Edited, designed and produced by The Studio Publishing Services Ltd
www.publishingservicesuk.co.uk
e-mail: studio@publishingservicesuk.co.uk

www.karnacbooks.com

CONTENTS

ACKNOWLEDGEMENTS

We wish to express our gratitude and thanks to our contributors, Dick Blackwell, Lionel Kreeger, Malcolm Pines, and Rocco Pisani for their thoughtful introductions and commentaries.

We wish to thank to Roberto Schöllberger for co-writing with Patrick de Maré a final paper in this book. Thanks also to Tom Ormay for writing an introduction to Patrick de Maré's and Roberto Schöllberger's papers on the mind, which were included in our original manuscript.

We wish to extend a special thanks to Yvonne Agazarian for her insightful preface and for her enthusiasm and guidance in helping us to bring the publication of this book to fruition.

For their technical assistance, we wish to thank Damaris Baker, Anthony Blake, and Jack Stefano.

Thanks also to Kuno Bachbauer, Diane Koslow, Beatrice Liebenberg, Nola Steinberg, and Isaiah Zimmerman for their support and encouragement throughout this process.

To our fathers, mothers, and mentors;
for their humanity and love

Yvonne M. Agazarian, EdD, FAPA, DFAGPA, CGP, is a clinical professor in the Postdoctoral Program in Group Psychotherapy, Adelphi University. She treats, teaches, trains, and consults in systems-centred practice. She developed the Theory of Living Human Systems, and founded the Systems-centered Training and Research Institute, whose training programme was awarded the best programme for 2010 by AGPA. She has authored and co-authored seven books and many articles. In 1997, she received the Group Psychologist of the Year Award from Division 49 of the American Psychological Association.

Dick Blackwell, BSc., CertEd, MInstGA, is a group analyst, family therapist, and organisational consultant in private practice. He has also worked at the Medical Foundation for the Care of Victims of Torture and Organized Violence for twenty years. He is a consultant with Centrepoint, working with homeless young people. He has specialised previously in work with suicide and psychosis, and has a special interest in culture and sport as an art form. A former chair of the Institute of Group Analysis, he was a member of Pat de Maré's large experimental group from 1976–1980.

Patrick de Maré, FRCPsych, was educated at St Cyprian's, Wellington College, Cambridge University, and St George's Hospital. In 1942, he was called up into the Royal Army Medical Corps and spent four years in the Army as a psychiatrist, working at the Northfield Military Hospital, where his mentors were Foulkes, Bion, and Rickman. He commanded the 21st Army Exhaustion Centre in Europe during the European Campaign 1944–1945. In 1952, he co-founded with S. H. Foulkes the Group Analytic Society and subsequently, with others, the Institute of Group Analysis and the Group Analytic Practice in London. He was the first consultant psychotherapist at St George's Hospital, London, and also worked as a consultant psychotherapist at Halliwick Hospital. In 1984, de Maré participated in establishing the Large Group Section in the Group Analytic Society of the Institute of Group Analysis. In the 1980s, he created the Median Group. In 1992, the Median Group Section was recognised as a separate section from the Large Group Section of the Group Analytic Society. Patrick de Maré is the author of *Perspectives in Group Psychotherapy* and *The History of Large Group Phenomena*. He is the co-author, with Lionel Kreeger, of *Introduction to Group Treatments in Psychiatry*, and a co-author, with Robin Piper and Sheila Thompson, of *Koinonia, from Hate through Dialogue to Culture in the Large Group*.

Lionel Kreeger, MB, BS, FRCP, FRCPsych, DPM, is a member of the Institute of Psychoanalysis and a founder member of the Institute of Group Analysis. He qualified in medicine at Guy's Hospital in 1949, with registrarships in medicine and neurology. He worked with the National Service RAMC and entered psychiatry in 1957. He was a consultant psychiatrist and psychotherapist at Halliwick Hospital from 1965 to 1973 and a consultant psychotherapist at the Tavistock Clinic until 1979, a member of the Group Analytic Practice from 1973 and an independent Freudian psychoanalyst from 1969. He was Editor of *The Large Group* (1975), and a collaborator with Pat de Maré at Halliwick and the Group Analytic Practice.

Rachel Lenn, MA, PhD, CGP, is a psychologist in private practice in Potomac, Maryland where she works with individuals, couples, families, and groups. She is also a consultant to government agencies, educational institutions and private corporations. She is a graduate of the National Group Psychotherapy Institute, the Advanced Group Psychotherapy Program and was a founding member of the Median Group at the Washington School of Psychiatry (2000–2006). She is a member of the National Registry of Certified Group Psychotherapists, the American Group Psychotherapy Association and the American Psychological Association. She is an alumna of The Center for Mind-Body Medicine, Washington, DC and a former board member of The Washington Society for Jungian Psychology.

Malcolm Pines, FRCPsych, MinstGA, is a founder member of the Institute of Group Analysis, London. He is past president of the International Association of Group Psychotherapy and past president of the Group-Analytic Society. He is a former editor of the journal *Group Analysis* and an editor of the *International Library of Group Analysis* series (published by Jessica Kingsley, London). He is a former consultant psychotherapist at Tavistock Clinic, Maudsley Hospital, St Georges Hospital, Cassel Hospital, and a former member of the British Psychoanalytic Society.

Rocco A. Pisani, MD, is a psychiatrist, neurologist, and group analyst. He was head of the Neuropsychiatric and Psychosomatic Outpatient Department from 1974 to 2004. He is a former Professor of Psychiatry and Group Psychotherapy at the Department of Neurological Sciences, University La Sapienza in Rome. He began practising small group analysis in 1981 and median group in 1991 at the university and in private practice. The Sessions of the Median Group at the Department of Neurological Sciences from 1991 to 2003 are collected in nineteen volumes.

Roberto Schöllberger, BPsych, is a training analyst at the Institute for Psychoanalyse Zuerich-Kreuzlingen in Germany and is also currently working with the Mental Health Centres of Azienda Sanitaria Bolzano in Italy. He has worked with Psichiatria Democratica, the movement that helped get asylums closed and made community psychiatry possible in Italy. He is a supervisor of teamwork in clinical and social psychology and also leads training sessions in group therapy and group work.

Karen Stefano, EdM, MA, LPC, is a practising psychotherapist and bio-energetic analyst. She is co-founder of DuVersity, a non-profit educational organisation through which she has convened median groups in the USA, the UK, Mexico, and China. She is a graduate of the Washington School of Psychiatry National Group Psychotherapy Institute and the Analytic–Somatic Psychotherapy programme in Berkley, California. She is a member of the American and International Group Psychotherapy Associations, the American Counseling Association and was a member of the Median Group at the Washington School of Psychiatry (2000–2006). She is also an artist and leads expressive therapy groups, drawing on the synergy of group psychotherapy and expressive arts therapies. She is in private practice in Charles Town, West Virginia and works with individuals, couples, families, and groups.

I am honoured to include *Small, Large, and Median Groups: The Work of Patrick de Maré* in The New International Library of Group Analysis. This is the first in what I hope will be a sub-series of publications of the work of the pioneers of group analysis. Many members of the founding generation were primarily clinicians and teachers, and they published comparatively little. Selecting, editing and introducing their various presentations to a new generation is an appropriate expression of veneration, which also provides an opportunity and a space for colleagues and students to make links with particular points of view in the service of their own professional development and the development of our profession.

This book was edited by Rachel Lenn and Karen Stefano, two group psychotherapists who were trained and who practise primarily in the USA. They recognised that Pat was very much his own man with many idiosyncrasies, and with his own intellectual style and philosophical point of view. In some way, he was a prophet in his own land. However, Rachel and Karen also recognised that Pat was a very democratic and politically radical thinker and clinician who was always concerned with those who lacked power and who lived at the margins of it, whose voices might be shrill and perhaps louder than necessary, but would always carry important messages and lessons. Pat was sceptical of patriarchal authority and the imposition of only one point of view. Hence, his appreciation of the importance of large groups and his particular manner of convening them in a non-directive, open, and responsive way.

As I (Hopper, 2000) have recounted in a *Festschrift* presented for Pat in a Special Issue of *Group Analysis* edited by Harold Behr, I first met Pat in the late 1960s, when he took medical responsibility for my first training case for the British Association of Psychotherapists under the auspices of the London Centre for Psychotherapy. Malcolm Pines was my supervisor. In my view, it was necessary to think about this young woman in terms of traumatic experience and feelings of helplessness, and the social unconscious with respect to gender identity. Although this perspective was different from what was officially expected in the psychoanalytical trainings at the time, Pat encouraged me to think independently. He said that a group analytical perspective was necessary for the integration of psychoanalysis and sociology.

In dialogue with Pat, he expressed his appreciation of my (Hopper, 1965) MSc thesis in sociology, in which I proposed that the relationship between frustration, aggressive feelings, and aggression was mediated by normative and structural constraints and restraints that originated in foundation matrices, for example, gender and class relations (Hopper, 2003). The assumptions about the death instinct and aggression that had come to define Kleinian psychoanalysis were much too limiting. In later discussions, I took the view that the Freudian notion of sublimation was an active process, based on displacement and symbolisation, and not a passive process. Nor did we agree about the overriding and virtually unqualified use of large groups as a therapeutic tool as opposed to a consultation tool, or a community social work tool—to be used in what Foulkes called "open air psychiatry". Similarly, although we agreed that the mind was not the same "thing" as the brain, we disagreed that the mind was best studied in the context of median groups, which I doubted had special parameters of their own. Pat did not really accept the importance of taking an open-systems perspective. When challenged about this, his eyes would not exactly glaze over, but he would begin to talk about the power implicit in the private ownership of land. However, we remained in overall agreement that personal maturation and maturity involved the socio-cultural notion of citizenship, and that the concept of the social unconscious was central to the development of group analysis (Hopper & Weinberg, 2011).

Shortly after I (Hopper, 1982) referred for the first time to Erich Fromm's (1963) essay "The revolutionary character", Pat invited Lionel Kreeger and I into his room at the Group Analytic Practice for tea and some chocolate roulade that his wife Turid had made over the weekend. Pat used six tea bags in one large cup, but did not dilute his tea with either milk or lemon. I remember him with affection and gratitude for his personal support and help in my professional life, not least for including me on the Editorial Board of *Group Analytic International Panel and Correspondence* (*GAIPAC*), the precursor of *Group Analysis*. As the Editor of *GAIPAC*, Pat was really in his element, fostering dialogue with colleagues and friends from all over the world, many of whom have contributed to this book. I am pleased to have helped to edit a previous draft of *Small, Large, and Median Groups: The Work of Patrick de Maré*, and to assist in its eventual publication.

Earl Hopper, PhD

References

Fromm, E. (1963). The revolutionary character. In: *The Dogma of Christ*. New York: Holt, Rinehart and Winston.

Hopper, E. (1965). Some effects of supervisory style: a sociological analysis. *British Journal of Sociology*, 16(3): 189–205. Reprinted in Hopper, E. (2003), *The Social Unconscious: Selected Papers*. London: Jessica Kingsley.

Hopper, E. (1982). Group analysis: the problem of context. *Group Analysis*, XV(2): 136–151.

Hopper, E. (2000). From objects and subjects to citizens: group analysis and the study of maturity. *Group Analysis*, 33(1): 29–34.

Hopper, E. (2003). *The Social Unconscious: Selected Papers*. London: Jessica Kingsley.

Hopper, E., & Weinberg, H. (Eds.) (2011). *The Social Unconscious in Persons, Groups, and Societies: Volume I: Mainly Theory*. London: Karnac.

Yvonne Agazarian

This book is a remarkable tribute to the memory of Pat de Maré. You will find in these pages a selection of his work that represents his new and different understanding of groups, both large and small, that has not only had a significant impact on the practice of group in his lifetime, but also a potential for revolutionising current thinking both now and in the future.

The editors are owed a great debt of gratitude for putting so much important work together. They have organised the book around three sections on the small, median, and large groups. What is particularly moving is that each section is introduced by some of Pat's closest friends and colleagues. These introductions are not only invaluable preparation for reading the articles of Pat's that follow, but are also a poignant tribute to the writers' lives, work, their thinking, and much happiness that came from their close relationship with Pat. The book ends with Pat's more recent work addressing the philosophical aspects of "mind", written in conjunction with his colleague Roberto Schöllberger: "as Socrates has formulated the soul, Descartes the thinking mind, Pat the Mind".

I first got to know Pat in the Tivoli Gardens in Copenhagen in 1985. What I remember best is how much we laughed, and when I reluctantly parted from him after dinner I left with warmth that is still with me as I share the terrible loss with his many friends and colleagues. It was in London in 1990 that I had my longest talks with Pat. I was immersed in developing a systems theory for group at the time, and was very excited that Pat also insisted that groups needed to be understood in terms of group variables and not confined to interpretations based on the more familiar psychodynamics. However, he dismissed, with little interest, my conviction that the small, median, and large groups were more similar than different. I was thinking system isomorphy. In Lionel Kreeger's introduction to the large group, it would seem that his thinking also moved in that direction when he writes, "I have myself wondered occasionally whether the dynamics of the median group are so different from those of a small or large group but I respect Pat's own enthusiastic conviction of its uniqueness . . .". I was not as gracious as Lionel, and tried to insist that Pat listen to my rationale: "All groups are systems," I said, "all exist in a hierarchy. Therefore they qualify as isomorphic systems, similar in structure and function." Pat's eyes seemed to get bluer! He lost all interest and changed the subject. Such a firm but gentle giant.

We also discovered that we both shared a life-long interest in communication and both had been influenced by Shannon (1964) and Lewin (1951). My major interest was in identifying the driving and restraining forces to the transfer of information that would influence how groups developed. Pat's interest was more universal. It was in Koinonia, "communion, fellowship, intercourse . . . from the . . . language Koin . . . which united pre-classical Greece . . . belonging to everybody because it belonged to nobody". Pat stated that the appropriate context to develop Koinonia was the median group (small groups being too vulnerable to family transferences and large groups too vulnerable to chaos). Pat wondered if it might take up to ten years to establish Koinonian dialogue.

I, on the other hand, claimed that by introducing certain norms of communication at the very beginning of a group, whether the group be small, median, or large, groups could develop the equivalent of his Koinonian communication within the first few hours of their life. I am referring here to the practice of introducing the systems-centred method of functional sub-grouping at the very beginning of every group, requiring members to join each other empathically and then to build on each other's ideas (Agazarian, 1997). This, I said, would contribute to the discrimination and integration of differences, which was, perhaps, both the necessary and sufficient condition for the survival, development, and transformation of all group systems.

Pat was interested in the idea, but felt it to be outside the tradition of the conductor. He pointed out that the group matrix, as the total communicational network, gets laid down in the course of time and gradually emerges as a result of group interactions. So whereas I was arguing that group size was not the major variable in achieving this, Pat was emphasising that the size was a variable of great impact and that the Median group was ideal for the development of Koinonic communication.

I was also, at that time, deeply involved in understanding (and reversing) the dynamics of scapegoating in groups, which I attributed to the failure of understanding normal human aggression that is universally aroused when confronted with unacceptable differences. I argued that by denying normal human aggression it was converted into hatred.

Pat gently introduced to me both the universality and the importance of—hatred!

> Hate . . . which in Greek also means grief . . . then constitutes the basis for psychic energy, which is transformed and expressed in the form of thinking dialogue and learning as distinct from an instinctual instinct. We have arrived at the conclusion that the (median) group constitutes a structure large enough to contain and transform hate for cultural purposes via the system of dialogue . . . and . . . through the containment of hate . . . the transformation of energy into the socializing process of impersonal friendship and dialogue.[1]

Pat, thus, transformed the understanding of hatred in groups from a destructive affect into a natural, inevitable response to frustration, an energy that carries high potential for both destructive and constructive transformation.

Much of our attitude towards human aggression is generated by our disapproval of it, and our disapproval is directly related to our superego fear of our unconscious potential. There is no question that we owe a great debt to Freud for his gift to us of the unconscious. But his gift came at a price. Superego pathology has long been connected to a nightmare of demonic ideas, colluding with the profound fear of the unconscious that is inevitable if the unconscious is to contain Thanatos as well as Eros. What is more, the common psychodynamic understanding of hatred is closely linked to the destructive superego and superego guilt. Freud claimed that the energy of the superego is derived from the id. It is at this theoretical point that Pat introduced a seminal difference. Pat's argument (that might well turn the world of psychology upside down) is that the energy of the superego is not derived from the id, nor is it biological, nor is hatred and superego guilt a necessary corollary. Whilst love *is* linked to Eros, hate *is not* linked to Thanatos. "Hate is not the adversary of Eros but the inevitable irreversible outcome of the frustration of Eros: if there is any adversary to Eros, it is . . . ananke . . . external necessity."

Thus, Pat transforms Freudian pessimism into optimism by reversing Freud's thesis that civilisation is built upon the passive renunciation of instinctual gratification. On the contrary, says Pat, "it is the active frustration of hate to which the evolution of culture owes it origins . . .". Whereas, for Freud, the solution is passive, for Pat it is active. "It has become . . . clear to us that hate, arising out of the frustrating situation of the larger group . . . provides the incentive for dialogue and becomes transformed, through dialogue, into the impersonal fellowship of Koinonia . . ."

In the meantime, however, we in the field of psychotherapy are living under the tyranny of the superego. Perhaps the most destructive misunderstanding is to fail to see the difference between superego pathology and normal human aggression. Human aggression is the potential energy fundamental to fuelling the flow of energy and information between all levels of human exchange. It is also the potential energy necessary to manage the inevitable frustrations that occur in everyday life. It is only when normal human aggression is viewed through the lens of the punitive superego that it becomes pathological.

All in all, the contribution of Pat's that has the most impact on me and, indeed, perhaps on the conductors and leaders of groups in the future, is his reinterpretation of superego hatred into the raw material for creative energy. Many groups live with the terrible consequences of misunderstanding hatred as if it is linked to human aggression, and linking the two give both a bad name. Framing as pathological what could be otherwise interpreted as normal human conflict has important clinical consequences. For example: the exogenous depression that comes from people turning the other cheek and turning their aggression back in on themselves; the superego criticism of sadism and masochism that prevents the conflicts that they contain to be explored without judgment; the "anger management techniques" that teach people to act nicely instead of acting out, without understanding that it is not just their angry hatred that is being modified but also their living energy. Perhaps most serious of all is the acquired fear of aggression. Fear of aggression goes hand in hand with fear of feeling, and fear of feeling is too often resolved by rationalisition. It might be common knowledge, but perhaps not common understanding, that feelings feel the same whether they are generated by thoughts or whether generated by our basic sensory experience of the world. From this confusion, communication norms develop that are manifested in anxiety-laden explanations of the past or present, repetitive stories about childhood, and a basic split between good and evil. When perception is based on projection, people become enmeshed in the anguish of personalising.

In summary, Pat's work is ground-breaking and mind-blowing, considering its implications for the management of hatred in groups. In this marvel of a book, it is not just Pat's deeply felt scholarship and scholarly references, nor just the "Koinonic" experience awaiting the readers, but for a single, significant reframing of the understanding of the dynamics of aggression and hatred that might permanently change the practice of group.

Note

1. Pat is not alone in understanding that the metabolising hatred into fellowship results in a different potential for communication. Bennis and Shepard (1956) translated Bion's basic assumptions into a group development model that is not included in the Foulksian tradition. They then defined the common group eruptions of hatred towards the leader as a barometric event that generated the transition from preoccupations with authority into the phase of intimacy. In my turn, I then translated their developmental model into a systems approach, calling their fulcrum event "the crisis of hatred", common to the development of all isomorphic systems, whether the system be the person, member, sub-group, or the group-as-a-whole (Agazarian, 1997).

References

Agazarian, Y. (1997). *Systems-Centered Therapy for Groups.* New York: Guilford, reprinted by Karnac.

Bennis, W. G., & Shepard, H. A. (1956). A theory of group development. *Human Relations, 9*(4): 415–437.

Lewin, K. (1951). *Field Theory in Social Science.* New York: Harper & Row.

Shannon, C. E., & Weaver, W. (1964). *The Mathematical Theory of Communication.* Urbana, ILL: University of Illinois Press.

Introduction

Rachel Lenn and Karen Stefano

The papers in this book represent a sampling of Patrick de Maré's writings over six decades from the 1960s until his death in 2008. De Maré, a British psychiatrist and founding father of group analysis, pioneered the small group's evolutionary offshoots, the large and median groups. Patrick de Maré was an active participant in the compilation of these papers, selecting the contributors to introduce the different phases of his work. Many of these writings have been previously published in journals that are not easily accessible, in the transcripts of conferences, and/or in books that are now out of print. These papers provide a historical framework of group analysis from the perspective of Patrick de Maré. They also represent an important shift in thinking about the role of groups as a way to both socialise the individual and humanise society.

Our interest in Patrick de Maré's work, which led to our compiling these papers, emerged from our participation in large and median groups and our subsequent work with de Maré in London and the USA. We invited him to the USA to participate in several conferences. Prior to his first visit, we, along with other colleagues, initiated what was to become a six-year median group of clinicians (mostly group psychotherapists), at the Washington School of Psychiatry, in

Washington, DC. De Maré's visits and his writings were important to our experiencing and understanding the median group process. Included in this manuscript are some of the papers we distributed to the median group members as we attempted to understand and experience the process together. Copying the papers for new members (our group numbered twenty-eight at its peak) became tedious, and so the idea of compiling them into one usable volume was born.

This book is divided into three sections, with papers reflective of each phase of de Maré's theoretical and practical applications to group. De Maré was involved in the development of all three modalities of group: small, large, and median. He saw each group as useful for exploring personality development and the enactment of psychic life. The Epilogue is followed by the Addenda, which includes Patrick de Maré's autobiography and an article written by de Maré's first group mentor, Basil Beaumont. It is our hope that by presenting a holistic view of de Maré's work, it will allow the reader to think as de Maré did, beyond the boundaries of group analysis to societal healing.

Small groups

S. H. Foulkes initiated small group analytic psychotherapy in the early 1940s. The group analytic movement flourished in response to the need for new treatments that could handle the large number of soldiers suffering from the disasters of the Second World War. Foulkes, Rickman, Bion, and de Maré participated in what came to be known as the "Northfield experiments", in which groups were instituted in the hospital to treat war trauma. In 1952, Patrick de Maré, with Foulkes, co-founded the Group-Analytic Society and subsequently, with others, the Institute of Group Analysis and the Group Analytic Practice in London. The contribution of these pioneers involved an integration of the social, cultural, and political dimensions into the treatment of mental illness. The articles in this section cover the history, theory, development, and application of group analytic psychotherapy. Malcolm Pines, a former editor of the journal, *Group Analysis*, and a founder member with Patrick de Maré of the Institute of Group Analysis and the Group Analytic Practice, introduces this section of de Maré's writings.

Large groups

In the 1970s, Patrick de Maré and Lionel Kreeger introduced the large group (30+) to the Second European Symposium on Group Analysis, based on their work in developing an inpatient therapeutic community at Halliwick Hospital. In 1973, at the European Workshop in Group Analysis, de Maré and Kreeger co-convened the daily large group, each working from different theoretical perspectives. De Maré's post-Oedipal focus on lateralisation and "humanising society" diverged from Kreeger's emphasis on pre-Oedipal object relations. De Maré and Kreeger went on to co-author *Group Treatment in Psychiatry*. The articles in this section describe large group as a tool for exploring the interface between psychotherapy and socio-therapy. De Maré felt that large group dynamics tend to naturally focus on socio-cultural and political awareness, while small group dynamics address familial concerns. The larger group also reflects the social unconscious and the collective culture. De Maré links the use of large group back to the ancient Greeks and the rise of democracy, with its emphasis on citizenship. In 1984, de Maré participated in establishing the Large Group Section of the Group Analytic Society. Lionel Kreeger, also a founder member of the Institute of Group Analysis, introduces this section of Patrick de Maré's work.

Median groups

Patrick de Maré created the median group (12–30 members) in the 1980s as a bridge or transitional space between the small psychotherapy and large group. While it is large enough to represent society, it is small enough for all members to see each other and participate. This structure offers an opportunity for members to think and talk with each other, thus providing a reflective mirror between individual minds and society. Median group lends itself to the exploration of societal concerns by providing an operational method for exploring one's social assumptions and social myths about ethnicity, gender, race, religion, social class, etc. Median group dialogue provides a vehicle for the disentangling and sorting out of one's cultural assumptions and projections.

A median group is facilitated, not led, by a non-directive convener. He/she supports the role of participants at the ego level,
encouraging dialogue and reflecting on the nature of social and
cultural pressures. As the group evolves, transferences (termed transposition by de Maré) become increasingly societal, with the group as
a whole rather than the convener serving as the transferential object.
The essence of the median group is non-hierarchical, reflective
dialogue. In "The median group and the psyche" (1994), de Maré
writes that

> ... the median group is a situation where the psyche can most freely
> and fully be exercised and is least trammeled by the rules imposed on
> it either by the family setting of the small group or the extensive
> massifying effect of society at large. (p. 20)

De Maré was optimistic about the potential of engaging consciousness and using one's mind to contain and transform strong feelings.
He believed that energy, when appropriately contained, provided the
currency for deeper, more reflective dialogue, leading to both
increased individuation and, ultimately, a sense of interdependence.
De Maré referred to the goal of median group dialogue as "Koinonia",
"impersonal fellowship" or communion with humankind. In this
era of globalisation, there appears to be a breakdown in communication between ethnic, political, and cultural groups. De Maré
saw the median group, with its emphasis on dialogue and reflective
mind, as a way for individuals and groups to move from mindlessness to mindfulness, from chaos and hate to understanding and
Koinonia.

The Median Group Section of the Group Analytic Society was born
out of the Large Group Section in 1992. This segment of Patrick de
Maré's writings is introduced by Rocco Pisani, an Italian psychiatrist
and group analyst, who came to know of de Maré's work when
engaged in the process of translating Foulkes' writings into Italian.
Pisani convened median groups of patients for fourteen years in the
Outpatient Department of Neurological Sciences of La Sapienza
University in Rome. He has deepened the analytical approach to the
median group. The median group as developed by de Maré is also
used with non-clinical populations, including educational systems,
governments, businesses, prisons, and the military.

The meeting of minds and the evolution of mindfulness

During his final years, de Maré thought and wrote about the "The primacy of the mind and the battle against mindlessness", the title of a talk he delivered at the Washington School of Psychiatry in Washington, DC, in 2001. In his emphasis on the mind and consciousness, de Maré added a new dimension to group analytic theory with its traditional focus on the unconscious. De Maré differentiated group dialogue from free and group association because of its reflective *vs.* instinctual quality. He saw median group dialogue as a vehicle for the "cultivation of consciousness" for "knowing things with other people". According to de Maré, it is in the "reflective think tank" of the median group process that dialogue transforms mindlessness into understanding and meaning. Group dialogue works to promote outsight and the expansion of social consciousness, thoughtfulness, and mindfulness. In one of his final papers, de Maré and Schöllberger (2004) write, "It took us two world wars to conclude that wars solve nothing. Whilst intelligence is widely held to be an intellectual defense against experiencing feelings, it costs nothing: thought through rather than fought through".

Patrick de Maré's final papers were written in collaboration with Roberto Schöllberger during the last five years of his life. One of these papers is included in the median group section of this book as it is relevant to his work with the median group, de Maré's final contribution to group practice. The others are more philosophical and focus on the "mind", which, for de Maré, encompasses the mind, body, and soul.

In his final paper, "An apologia for the human mind" (2008), de Maré and Schöllberger write about the pre-eminence of the mind throughout history and culture, moving with ease and erudite knowledge through centuries and disciplines. De Maré and Schöllberger identify the Golden Rule of the Perennial Philosophy (love the other as oneself), as constituting "the essence of humanization". They state that without it we behave in a "subhuman way", without distinguishing between good and evil. In their study of the mind, de Maré and Schöllberger move from the Greeks to Patanjali, who wrote the original yogic text describing the mind, to Buddha, who, when asked what he was, responded, "I am awake".

Patrick de Maré was awake to the end, thinking, writing, and encouraging us through his work to also awaken and become conscious, to take responsibility for ourselves, each other, and our world. At ninety-two, after many years of clinical practice, de Maré came to view the mind and its evolution as essential for human transformation and our survival on the planet.

Epilogue

Dick Blackwell writes the Epilogue. A former Chair of the Institute of Group Analysis in London, Dick Blackwell first met Patrick de Maré in 1975 at the Institute of Group Analysis. As a student in the advanced programme, he participated in the Institute's first large group, which Patrick de Maré convened. In the Epilogue, Blackwell writes,

> One of [de Maré's] most profound observations is that the sort of dialogue that we need for genuine democracy is a skill, an art that has to be learnt; we cannot learn it from books but only by practising it in groups, large, or, at least, median groups."

Addenda

Harold Behr notes in the Editorial Introduction to the Special Issue of *Group Analysis*, *33*(1), dedicated to Dr Patrick de Maré, that de Maré's "passion for groups as a force for social change antedates his collaboration with Foulkes". Patrick de Maré's introduction to, and inspiration for, group work evolved through his affiliation with The Society for Creative Psychology. The organisation's founder, Basil Beaumont, in his 1935 pamphlet, *The Technique of Group Work* (reprinted in the Addenda), describes the principles and guidelines of this Society, whose aim was to understand group process through the practice of free and open discussion. De Maré attributes the origins of his life long engagement with group work to his affiliation with this Society. Also included in the addenda is Patrick de Mare's autobiography.

A man of panoramic vision, deep humanity, and great spirit, de Maré reminds us that Plato considered "Dialogue" (not war) the Supreme Art. It is with love and deep respect for Patrick de Maré and his ideas that we share this compilation of his writings.

References

Beaumont, B. (1935). *The Technique of Group Work: Society for Creative Psychology*. London: Favil Press.

Behr, H. (2000). Editorial introduction: Special issue: Dr. Patrick de Maré. *Group Analysis*, 33(1): 5–7.

De Maré, P. (1994). The median group and the psyche. In: D. Brown & L. Zinkin (Eds.), *The Psyche and the Social World: Developments in Group Analytic Theory* (pp.202–210). London: Jessica Kingsley.

De Maré, P., & Schöllberger, R. (2004). A case for mind. *Group Analysis*, 37(3): 339–352.

De Maré, P., & Schöllberger, R. (2008). Apologia for the human mind. *Group Analysis*, 41(1): 5–30.

Patrick de Maré, Hampstead, London, UK circa 1980.

PART I
SMALL GROUPS

"Group-analytic psychotherapy is a method of group psycho-therapy initiated by myself from 1940 onwards in private psychiatric practice and out-patient clinics. It grew out of, and is inspired by, my experience as a psychoanalyst, but also it is *not* a psychoanalysis of individuals in a group. Nor is it the psychological treatment of a group by a psychoanalyst. It is a form of psychotherapy *by* the group *of the* group, including its conductor. Hence the name 'Group Analytic Psychotherapy'."

(Foulkes, quoted in de Maré, 1983, p. 229)

"Basically the contribution of Foulkes and Northfield was the handling of a new dimension; the social, the cultural and the political in relationship to neurosis . . . I realize today that what I witnessed there was a man vitalized by the discovery of this crucial issue, of the link between the deepest 'vertical' levels of the intrapersonal psychoanalytic with its 'horizontal' transper-sonal social context."

(de Maré, 1983, pp. 228–229)

Reference

De Maré, P. (1983). Michael Foulkes and the Northfield Experiment. In: M. Pines (Ed.), *The Evolution of Group Analysis* (pp. 218–231). London: Routledge & Kegan Paul.

Introduction to small groups

Malcolm Pines

I have always regarded Patrick de Maré as a man ahead of his time, able to envisage and then to pull together the skeins of wide ranging psychological, philosophical, and historical ideas. The two main papers in this section are written in the 1960s and there is still much to be learnt from our gleanings from his theoretical fields.

The paper "Non-transference elements in group psychotherapy" is undated. It is a more than adequate account of Foulkes' model of group psychotherapy given to an international congress where many different approaches are being debated. The originality of de Maré's own thinking appears when he is giving the wider context: the first and second scientific revolutions; Lewin's field theory; cybernetics and information theory; the transference from energy to information. This paper, which conveys de Maré's wide-ranging intellect and interest, is invaluable, as it conveys more clearly than did Foulkes himself the pulse of the time. His own language begins to appear when he writes, "Ego training is an active and a corrective experience, not by the analyst but by the slowly emerging group network, which becomes progressively more complex, sophisticated and affiliative as distinct from hierarchical". "A profound modification takes place in the superego once it becomes, as it were, the property of the group, which is then translated from the primitive archaic authoritarian institution by communication to a socialising group matrix". His capacity to range widely and then hold things together is evident in the many diagrams, which he later on was able to draw.

De Maré's freedom to range widely can be attributed partly to his not signing on to the psychoanalytic movement after his personal analysis with Dr Karen Stephen, who, with her husband, Adrian Stephen, were early members of the Psychoanalytical Society.

There is much of interest in the paper, "Some theoretical concepts in group psychotherapy", from 1963. His opening sentence has a bold ring:

> The salient feature of group analytic psychotherapy lies in the intro-duction of a manoeuvrable social dimension, in the form of the group matrix, into the fabric of the actual technique itself. Any approach to group therapy that fails to do this not only fails to do justice to the therapeutic potential of the group, but might, indeed, become actively anti-therapeutic.

He introduces the term, "group locus", which nowadays we term the "group setting", and indicates that it will undergo various fantasy meanings but still remain "a suspended transitional 'proxy' entity". He introduces us to *plurality*: to the relative freedom with which the individual-in-the-group and his inner perspective can gain expres-sion. This plurality acts like a sounding board, enhancing the latent discursive potentials of the group members, gradually evolving into the total communicative network, the group matrix.

His next paragraph is a thoughtful account of the evolving change processes as individuals emerge as foreground figures against the evolving group matrix. He finds more use than does Foulkes for Freud's group psychology of the primal horde, that group analysis can bring about a social resolution of the family constellation and the Oedipus complex.

> The primitive authoritarian conductor-centred configuration of the initial phases with the leader–group cleavage gradually gives way and is taken over by the emerging group matrix, the social solution to the Oedipal conflict. . . .

When the group, then in its initial phases of a family configuration, combines with the help of the binding power of the matrix to take over its social, as opposed to family, function, the decision is guilt free and represents a reduction in tension and hostility between the members themselves, also between themselves and the conductor, who is then seen in his socially "real" role. This also occurs intrapersonally between the ego and superego, which, in the course of this steady take-over, become mutually modified in such a way as to function syntonically.

The steady take-over then from the rigidly authoritarian/chaos quality by a progressively evolving matrix that permeates intrapersonal as well as intragroup (transpersonal) dimensions represents the very essence of the therapy.

I do not know of anyone else who has so thoughtfully pondered over and illuminated the gradual evolution of the therapeutic potential of the group, eloquently summarising and giving us much to ponder over.

These papers were written before Yalom's major work, *The Theory and Practice of Group Psychotherapy* (1970), which since then has gone into five editions. During these years, psychoanalysis has evolved with Kohutian self-psychology, relational psychoanalysis and attachment based theory and practice. It has moved from being based, in John Rickman's terms, on one body psychology towards two and multiple body psychologies. Close scrutiny of transference-countertransference processes has established the importance of the intersubjective essence of the human psyche. Psychoanalysis is indeed now much more founded on a group psychology. What all this is leading to is well represented in a paper by Lyons-Ruth (1999). She writes that psychoanalytic theory moves increasingly towards a relational intersubjective and social constructivist stance. The subjectivities of patient and analyst contribute to the form and content of the dialogue that emerges between them. There is a shift to a more fluid and neutral view of therapy processes; therefore, there is also a need for a psychology model of development that converges with this. Psychoanalysis now studies non-interpretative mechanisms of change. Knowing how to do things with others, that is, integrate a semantic and affective meaning with behavioural and interactive procedures, is the essential process of developing a sense both of the mind of the self and the mind of the other. "Theory of mind" is a subject of intense interest and research. Whether starting in early childhood or adulthood, one must first elaborate an awareness of how one's own mental life is both similar to and different from that of others, to elaborate further in understanding of how to make these similarities and differences explicit in dialogue, to construct procedures for negotiating with the other(s) in the face of differences, which are all essential features of the group analytic situation.

I think it is a feature of the time in which these papers were written that the concept of empathy is not discussed. Empathy weaves a web of connection that supports and contains our mental and emotional lives. De Maré was a member of Foulkes' original group of colleagues, which included Norbert Elias. Norbert pointed out that we live our lives in chains of interdependency, figurations, as he called them, and that we need each other if we are to survive physically, mentally, and effectively. The strength of empathy arises from commitment to truthful self-knowledge and truthful understanding of others. Through this search for truth, we protect ourselves from self-deception and from deception by others. Group analytic psychotherapy gives to us and to our patients opportunities to see ourselves more clearly, to understand others more accurately, to communicate our perceptions in sensitive and tactful ways.

In 1998, thirty-five years after de Maré's paper titled "Non-interpretative mechanisms", Daniel Stern and the Boston group for the study of change published an important paper, "There's something more than interpretation: non-interpretative mechanisms of psychoanalytic theory". Its opening sentence is, "It is by now generally accepted that something more than interpretation is necessary to bring about therapeutic change". They are applying learning from infant observation and emphasise that in infancy mutual state regulation between infant and care-giver is a fundamental vital process, involving attunement, apprehension, and recognition, which will "among other factors determine the nature and coherence of the infant's experience". They then apply this model to the process of psychotherapy, where regulation arises out of mutual efforts, constant struggles, negotiating, missing, and repairing, and mid-course correcting, scaffolding, processes with which we are familiar in the group setting, where there is always an intersubjective process in mutual recognition, mutual empathy, and mutual empowerment. The model that they apply to these processes of moving along and *moments of meeting* is that of non-linear dynamic systems that produce emergent properties. The "open space" presents new possibilities, openings to new levels in intersubjectivity. Moving along consists of sequences of *now moments* arriving at the *kairos* moments, the propitious moment from which change can emerge. These moments of meeting are moments of healing connection; the rhythm of connection, disconnection, pause, reconnection; connection, pause for thought, and feeling; reconnecting on a new basis. Foulkes foresaw these developments with his emphasis on mirroring, resonance, the primacy of communication over interpretation, the mutual processes of introjection and projection, internalisation of experience in relationships, and the group as matrix of the individual's mental life.

In one of his final papers, Foulkes writes that, "The therapist is akin to a poet, who finds a way to recognise and express deeper meanings as does the poet express his motives in society". These words fit so well to the work of Patrick de Maré, who is, in so many ways, a poet of group analysis, a far-seer throughout his life as a psychotherapist.

His other two papers, on Northfield and Major Bion, are valuable, sensitive vignettes of Northfield, where both Foulkes and Bion forged their theories from the intense experience of an army at war. Patrick de Maré and James Anthony are our witnesses to these founding moments.

References

Lyons-Ruth, K. (1999). The two person unconscious: intersubjective dialogue, enactive relational representation, and the emergence of new forms of relational organization. *Psychoanalytic Inquiry*, 94(19): 576–617.

Yalom, I. D. (1970). *The Theory and Practice of Group Psychotherapy*. New York: Basic Books.

CHAPTER ONE

Some theoretical concepts in group analytic psychotherapy*

Patrick de Maré

The salient feature of group analytic psychotherapy lies in the introduction of a manoeuvrable social dimension, in the form of the group matrix, into the fabric of the actual technique itself. Any approach to group therapy that fails to do this not only fails to do justice to the therapeutic potential of the group, but might, indeed, become actively anti-therapeutic.

Group analysis offers us a field in which the interplay between the part and the whole with the emergent evolution of the new can be seen in continuous operation. Gestalt theory took the view that the wholeness property is given rather than evolved from the combination of simpler elements. In group analytic psychotherapy, we see an extension of this, which is *first* the existence of relatively autonomously functioning individuals; second, their interaction with each other, and *finally*, as a result of this, the laying down of a network of communication that establishes the contours of a discrete "whole" group identity, which Foulkes has called the group matrix. This

---

*This unpublished paper was first presented to the International Congress of Group Psychotherapy, Milan, in 1963.

matrix comes to play a highly significant role in the therapeutic process. Development then follows along the lines of a chaos–logos–cosmos cycle of events roughly equivalent to the structure, process, and content of the group.

Foulkes adopts an inductive approach and avoids arriving at premature formulations. It favours a tentative orientation, admittedly less easy to define, but preferable to more facile models that bring distortion in their wake. The fact that the group continues to elude adequate definition stands us in good stead, for it acts as a reminder that concepts of group analysis "must be independent and not borrowed ones". In this respect, it is refreshing to note, in an article, published by Foulkes as early as 1944, that he tentatively pointed out the therapeutic factors as being:

(a) the social and group situation
(b) a collection of factors which can be conveniently grouped under the inclusive heading of communication, for example, mirror reaction, activation, and exchange.

These foreshadowed much of what later became further elaborated, with the notable exception of the concept of the group matrix, which was not actually described in publication, I think I am correct in saying, until 1957, when it was acknowledged as being "at the centre of all our thinking about groups".

In the group analytic situation, in which group psychotherapy is observed in its "purest and least contaminated form, the accent is entirely on the free and spontaneous action and interaction within the group with as little interference, interpretive or other, as possible". There is the triad of, first, the small primary group itself with its "T" set of factors, which is distinguished not so much by "the presence of certain unique factors but a particular combination of several factors and the way in which they are used"; second, of the process of communication of "all observable responses", and third, of the group matrix, "the total communicationable network".

The group analytic situation is best reserved as a comprehensive term covering all three constructs of the triad. To date, most of our attention has been taken up by attempts to understand the first of the triad, the small group itself, in its initial phases, its establishment, its framework, selection, procedure, to observe its special features, etc. To cover all these aspects, I should like to introduce two main headings under which it is (I hope) possible to reduce and clarify the complexities of the small primary group itself.

The first heading is the *group locus*. It consists of the basic matters of general group arrangements, size, selection, and procedure. It is, in fact, the relatively standardised and unchanging framework. Once established, the group locus exercises considerable influence upon all subsequent events, reducing interference from outside sources (including the conductors) to a minimum. It takes on various phantasy meanings at various stages, depending on changes in the configuration of the matrix at any particular moment, for instance, the family, the stage, the forum, the community. It remains a suspended, transitional, "proxy" entity, quasi-fantasy, quasi-real, equivalent to the analyst in the psychoanalytic situation. With its a-programmatic occupation, the locus can be compared to a stage, but without a set play, or a law court without a legal code.

The group locus is constantly faced by the dilemma of having to remain sufficiently encapsulated to provide protection from the usual social involvements, which enables the members to feel they can afford to drop their defensiveness. On the other hand, it has to borrow some of the authority of the outside community to give the group sufficient weight to stand up to the censorious and predatory nature of neurosis.

The boundaries of the group locus have been compared to a semipermeable membrane, which protects the group both from the disturbing influences within the surrounding environment and from the endopsychic phantasmagoria of the individual members. Within this locus the members should feel free to adopt, shed, assign, and test out various social or, alternatively, phantasy roles, various personifications of impulses, trends, or traits in free speculation.

The second heading, also referring to the small group itself, is its *plurality*, covering specifically the more "chaotic" collective nature of the group. In a recent paper, Dr Salomon Resnik talks of "the constitutional plurality of the group situation", and comments that "any group implies plurality of objects which is what characterises the group as such".

This is more than a play on words, for it not only *counters* any tendency towards a too facile reductive rendering of the group-as-a-whole, such as regarding "the total material produced by *all* the members of the group as if it had been produced by one member in an individual session", or anchoring the group to over-simplified models such as the family, the breast, or the community, but emphasises the relative freedom with which the individual-in-the-group and his inner perspective can gain expression.

Because Foulkes has refrained from emphasising either the pluralistic at the expense of the holistic features or vice versa, he has been represented as attempting to establish an uneasy compromise between psychoanalysis and gestalt psychology. This is tantamount to saying that because he is not prepared to discard either of these perspectives, he is making a compromise. Even if this were so, it would be preferable to excluding any of the delicate emerging processes. In fact, we should be prepared to collate all that has been fathered from allied disciplines rather than imposing idiosyncratic versions. For instance, there is much in his approach that bears affinities with the existential outlook, the "being-in-the-world" relates to the individual-in-the-group, "encounter" with confrontation. There is also the emphasis on action communication and intimacy, but in a social setting, "ego training in action", and in the concept of the group matrix, historical and temporal and spatial dimensions play their roles. The social situation of the group brings out real anxiety and real guilt in most cogent ways, and the individual, in finding he can no longer hide, discovers his *Dasein*. The subject–object cleavage very obviously loses its consequence in the group situation, in keeping with other dichotomies, for instance the leader–group cleavage.

Like a sounding board, the plurality within the group enhances salient trends already inherent in the individual personality, for example, splitting, projection (and projective identification), and introjection, for it offers opportunities for dramatisation, personification, polarisation, amplification, and multiple representation, with temporal, spatial + historical sequences that gradually evolve a group matrix, the total communicational network.

On the other hand, the binding power of the matrix leads to a restructuralisation and eventual re-socialisation within its network. This is itself, in turn, being continuously modified, the pluralistic foreground figures being highlighted, "located", in their particular configuration against the background of the emerging group matrix. The matrix, therefore, lies in an antithetical relationship to the plurality of the group.

The conductor also bears an interesting relationship to the matrix. As the matrix waxes, his function wanes, and leadership quality as a function of the group is delegated in varying ways, the undivided leader throughout being the total group. The conductor attempts to be perceptive to the group's leadership constellation, ranging from the didactic to the heuristic. The group, in learning to operate as-a-whole and with the help of the progressively emerging group matrix, is able to take over its own leadership function without feeling divided and without guilt. This is reminiscent of certain passages from *Totem and Taboo* (Freud, 1919), for example, "the sense of guilt. This can only be allayed through the solidarity of all the participants . . .", or "together they dared and accomplished what would have remained impossible for them singly" . . . "the memorable criminal act which so many things began, social organisation, moral restrictions and religion". ". . . A change has really taken place in the form of society, from father horde to the brother clan".

The primitive authoritarian conductor-centred configuration of the initial phases with the leader–group cleavage gradually gives way and is taken over by the emerging group matrix, the social solution to the Oedipal conflict.

Unlike most other leadership situations, the conductor does not attempt to block this transformation, but fosters the growing complexity of the matrix *pari passu* with his own "decrescendo". This one attempts to achieve, in group analytic psychotherapy, as smoothly and evenly as possible. It can, in fact, *only* be achieved as a result of the work done in the process of learning to communicate and in the course of, often considerable, time, motivated by "this creative sense of guilt which has not become extinct with us".

Selection here plays a paramount role in enabling both the group and conductor to facilitate the process of learning that the potential leader throughout is the total group who guides the conductor. He, in his turn, responds and guides the group, and it is up to him to harness this symbiosis for therapeutic purposes rather than perpetuate the leader–group cleavage.

Freud described the primary group as "a number of individuals who have substituted one and the same object for their ego ideal and have consequently identified themselves with one another in their ego". For the group analytic psychotherapist, this is a preliminary phase in the group's history, a group without a matrix. He also commented that the family was a reconstruction of the former primal horde, which restores a great part of their former rights to the fathers.

When the group, then in its initial phases of a family configuration, combines with the help of the binding power of the matrix to take over its social, as opposed to family, function, the decision is guilt free and represents a reduction in tension and hostility between the members themselves, also between themselves and the conductor, who is then seen in his socially "real" role. This also occurs intrapersonally between the ego and superego, which, in the course of this steady take-over, become mutually modified in such a way as to function syntonically.

On the other hand, if this does not occur, for example, when the take-over is by another member in isolation, distortions occur, such as the appearance of the "mad leader" on the scene, which are not necessarily inevitable group phenomena. This would seem to denote an unevenness in the growth of the matrix and a breakdown in smooth communication, for instance, when the conductor withdraws prematurely, before a sufficient matrix has been established. This breakdown might also occur at any time, however late in the proceedings, when the group is faced by a shared problem of incommunicability. Examples of this include a shared neurotic disturbance, typically when the constellation is changing from a homosexual to a heterosexual pattern, or when the men and women are encountering prohibitions in exchanging with each other. At these points, they may evince the recurrence of a leader-centred but hostile pattern of behaviour; they share a phantasy that the conductor objects to this exchange, or else that the other members will object or reject, which prevents their testing it out.

This steady take-over, then, from the rigidly authoritarian/chaos quality by a progressively evolving matrix that permeates intrapersonal as well as intragroup (transpersonal) dimensions represents the very essence of the therapy. The dilemma for the group-analytic psychotherapy group is that the conductor does not identify with the manoeuvres imposed on him by a group in a rudimentary state of communication.

These comments cover only the first and third aspects of the triad, the second, that dealing with the processes of activation, motivation, and communication, closely involves the role of the conductor and is more a subject on its own about which, perhaps, least is known; certainly it is the most complex.

Summary

An attempt is made to systematise certain basic concepts surrounding the notion of the group-analytic psychotherapeutic situation. Its unique contribution lies in the introduction of a manoeuvrable social dimension into the actual fabric of the technique itself. Its processes can be viewed from a triad of three main constructs along the lines of a sort of chaos–logos–cosmic sequence.

I. The first of the triad is the small primary group that starts off in a state of relative communicational confusion and that, relatively speaking, demands to be organised. It has striking characteristics, which can be placed under two main headings:

(a) The group locus, which is the general unchanging framework of the members, their number, selection, and the general arrangements and procedure.

(b) The group plurality, whose diversity is an essential feature of the small group, mobilising such characteristic processes as role-playing, personification, polarisation, amplication, multiple representation, etc.

II. The second aspect of the triad includes the processes of activation, communication, and motivation. This aspect is only briefly touched upon as being the most complex and as being a subject on its own.

III. The third construct of the triad is the group matrix, the total communicational network that is laid down in the course of time and gradually emerges as a result of the group's interaction. It is, in fact, the group's manoeuvrable social dimension, which, as it evolves, comes to play an increasingly significant role in the therapeutic process. It modifies very crucially the conductor's function with a dissolution of the leader–group and subject–object cleavage, the group's equivalent to a social resolution of the family constellation and the Oedipus complex.

References

Foulkes, E. (Ed.) (1990). *Selected Papers of S. H. Foulkes: Psychoanalysis and Group Analysis*. London: Karnac.

Foulkes, S. H. (1948). *Introduction to Group-Analytic Psychotherapy: Studies in the Social Integration of Individuals and Groups*. London: Maresfield Reprints, 1983.

Freud, S. (1919). *Totem and Taboo*, A. A. Brill (Trans.). New York: Moffat, Yard and Company.

Freud, S. (1921c). *Group Psychology and the Analysis of the Ego. S.E., 18*: 67–143. London: Hogarth.

Resnik, S. (1995). *Mental Space*. London: Karnac.

CHAPTER TWO

Michael Foulkes and the Northfield experiment*

Patrick de Maré

I first met Michael Foulkes thirty-three years ago at Northfield, during the hot summer of 1944 just before D-Day. Writing this brings back these memories with a particular poignancy. His death at the age of seventy-seven from a heart attack was painless and occurred suddenly in the middle of answering a question at a seminar of close colleagues. He had already asked me a few weeks previously to write about Northfield, and I am filled with the sad realisation that the opportunity to have heard his comments is lost forever; lost, too, is the theoretical companion to his last book, which was published in 1975, which he was in the process of preparing.

My first meetings with him were brief, since I was en route to Normandy. He was, in fact, the only person who witnessed the "Northfield experiment" throughout, from his instituting it in July 1943 to his demobilisation in December 1945. Even so, in the middle of the enormous tensions of war just before D-Day and before getting to know him as well as I did later, I was very aware of a feeling of

*Previously published in 1983 by Routledge and Kegan Paul, in M. Pines (Ed.) *The Evolution of Group Analysis* (pp. 218–230).

intense excitement that surrounded his whole personality. He seemed to transcend the conditions of those oppressive days and sparked off in those associated with him an enduring inspiration and enthusiasm. It was not simply the charisma of an original and creative thinker that I think we all recognised, but the impact of contact with a mind that far exceeded in depth and breadth any that we had had the good fortune to come across before. This was coupled with the fact that he was in the throes of creating a dimension which was to affect the whole subsequent course of psychotherapy, for, in introducing the psycho-social level by an actual operative technique that could be simply applied, he succeeded in turning the whole direction of psychotherapy towards a new dimension. In asking us to look at the other side of the coin, which, until then, had been unacknowledged, that is, the context within which a psychotherapeutic relationship might or might not occur, he drew our attention to this new and crucial issue, made particularly apposite by the very circumstances in which we found ourselves: war.

Northfield was a building with enormously long corridors so that, busy and pressured by his daimon as he was, he seemed always to be on the trot. He was compactly built, his movements were quick and light and he was an excellent tennis player. He had considerable charm and was good looking in a puck-like way, with greying hair and extraordinary grey-blue eyes. He had a powerful but fine Jewish nose and sensuous lips; his teeth were set widely apart, and he would often smile with a slightly mischievous expression. He spoke English with a German accent but with an extremely good command of words, since he was keenly interested in the appropriate choice of words. He would struggle for hours at a time over a particular term— for instance, the use of the word "catalyst" or "matrix" or "group-analytic psychotherapy", which was the name he finally assigned to his technique. Once he had become involved with a topic, which was very often, he talked in a breathless way, breaking off with an occasional sigh, when he might look down at the floor, become quiet and absorbed (and I would wonder if he was bored by some comment that had been made). In addressing a person, he would turn his head and look at them fully and directly and gave the impression of concentrating his entire attention on what they were saying. In fact, his capacity for concentration was enormous, but (I think) he found it extremely tiring. For instance, once, in a group, a certain author had said that the book he had embarked on needed only a further fort-night's work to be completed. "Only a fortnight's work!" gasped Michael. He had written his first book during a fortnight's holiday in 1947, more or less without a break, smoking continuously, and at the end of it he had his first, fortunately slight, heart attack.

He felt passionately about ideas; for him there was no facile split between intelligence and feeling and he appeared to feel with his thoughts and think with his feelings, as if thinking were an instinctive, enjoyable process. If someone said something that interested him, his whole body seemed to move forward, as if he could actually see his ideas. When he was involved in a discussion, he would talk with a rush of words, half-thoughts, and free associations, in a sort of confu-sion to which he would allow full range. To people's consternation, he would sometimes lecture like this, baring his mind, allowing himself to be confused, worrying over an idea. In discussions, he would continue tirelessly in this style, sometimes for hours, which could be exhausting to others as well as to himself. Finally, matters might either be left in the air, when he would be both dissatisfied and apologetic, or, alternatively, he would suddenly punctuate the flow of thoughts with some startlingly clear conclusion, as if this had been obvious to him all along.

He would pick people's brains blatantly but would be more than happy if they returned the compliment. His manner was quiet and gentle and I never once saw him angry or harassed, but he would occasionally be ruined by an idea. Sometimes he would ask a discon-certing or enigmatic question, the reply to which would appear to dis-appoint him, and this slightly ironical or mischievous smile would appear in his expression; sometimes, on the other hand, he would jump at an idea and would be flatteringly pleased. He hardly ever stopped thinking and planning, yet his thinking clearly tired him, and he would rub his eyes with thumb and forefinger and blink as if the brightness of his ideas was exhausting.

The first time I met him was in a consulting room at Northfield. It was shortly after I had seen him in the distance at one of the long tables in the dining room, talking to Martin James. It was a sunny spring day and he was standing over some coloured powder paints (for he said, in passing, that he was interested in certain colour tests). The impression he gave was of lightness, happiness, and excitement, and I found myself fascinated by the way he talked, by the refreshing way in which he put things, a feeling of originality and pleasure and of personal friendliness. But I was not prepared for the feeling of intense liking that I had for him. He was forty-five at the time and I was twenty-eight. In the course of conversations, this faintly mysterious smile of his would often flit across his face and there would be this ironical inflection in the tone of his answer, which might be followed by a short humorous laugh. For instance, on one occasion, in describing people's contributions to a discussion, he commented, "You know, some of the things they were saying made no sense, people often seem to get seriously preoccupied with absolute rubbish", and he gave this laugh, which had a peculiarly unprejudiced warmth and gave an impression of complete acceptance of them as people.

God knows what he thought of me. I do know we had a mutual regard and friendliness. I was both a communist and a Roman Catholic and I had started a personal psychoanalysis with Karin Stephen a year before the war. I was deeply interested in groups, in which I had participated in London and Cambridge as a medical student during the 1930s. He was obviously amused by some of my more glaring inconsistencies, but he never scoffed at them. Indeed, he seemed to enjoy arguing through some of my dilemmas and agreed "in principle" (a phrase he often used) with some of my more radical views, particularly about banking and the economic system. Of all people, as a refugee he had reason to be sensitive to the political implications of war. I would argue that adjusting to reality implied adjusting to a status quo, in this instance a highly wasteful war. He had been in the German army in the First World War, and here he was with the British Forces in the Second World War. The issues of fascism, communism, and democracy were at stake and it was only a matter of chance that we found ourselves on the side of the "goodies". He would tease me by saying that he had not yet analysed a communist whose political stance was not based on some form of neurotic conflict. He pointed out that we were not an experimental or research unit, but a military hospital working under high pressure, where the practical needs of the day had to be met. His attitude towards the Nazis was that of the psychoanalysts in Berlin who had declared that "in good times we treat them and in bad times they rule us".

In fact, during the early 1930s, before leaving Germany in 1933, Michael had been acquainted with members of a Marxist sociological group called the Institute of Social Research, which included

Horkheimer, Fromm, Adorno, and Marcuse and which has since become known as the Frankfurt School. They attempted to integrate Marxist theory with that of psychoanalysis. Their institute was in the same university building as the Institute of Psychoanalysis (in Frankfurt). Marcuse, who was a somewhat younger man, bore a striking physical resemblance to Michael.

Although the idea of groups had been very much in the air in London of the mid 1930s, Foulkes had little notion of the movements associated with them. Apart from gestalt, field, and holistic theory, two papers in the mid 1920s by Trigant Burrow in which the phrase "group analysis" was first used (and of whom Foulkes said, "He was the first person to put the group into the centre of this thinking. That was and remains his great merit"), two plays, one by Pirandello and the other by Gorki, and the two psychoanalysts Wender and Schilder working in the USA, he had to rely on his own resources for inspiration, and he had no direct sources of information other than the situation at Northfield itself.

The story of Foulkes' first attempts to apply group therapy in 1940 is interesting. In the late 1930s, he had often considered how rewarding it would be if his patients in analysis were to hear each other's free associations. He had always looked upon psychoanalysis in the light of life as a whole, and not upon life from the perspective of the analytic couch. Finally, in 1940, in the waiting-room of his private practice in Exeter, he decided to invite his patients to carry out as far as possible "free associations" in a free-flowing dialogue. It was there, after his first session, held in a waiting-room at 23 Dix's Field, that he felt a historical event had taken place in psychiatry. "But," he added afterwards to his wife, "nobody knows about it."

After two years' work with fifteen patients in a group, he published a joint paper in 1942 with Eve Lewis, a psychologist.

The concrete realisation of the part that social conditions play in their troublesome problems, the social front of inner conflicts, so to speak, gets people thinking in a critical way and makes them experience the part they themselves are playing, both actively and passively, as objects as well as instruments of these condition, an altogether desirable contribution to their *education as responsible citizens* in participating in a free and democratic community.

The reciprocal significance of the individual and the group was already discovered.

In the same paper they mention group association as distinct from "free association", and go on to point out that the specifically group features are socialisation, sharing, stimulation, and exchange, and that the therapist slowly shifts his attention to *the group situation as the preferred frame of reference* (my italics here and above).

In 1942, before Foulkes was called up and, therefore, before his arrival at Northfield in 1943, there had already been a preliminary attempt made by Majors Bion and Rickman to establish a group approach in one of the wards (and which I witnessed peripherally). This had lasted for about six weeks. I had been sent with some twelve other psychiatrists to a six-month course in military psychiatry, which Bion and Rickman conducted. (Five were American, one was Polish and six were British.) During these six months, which were extremely stimulating and which mainly took the form of seminars, Bion and Rickman had launched the "first Northfield experiment", as it came to be called. A ward was set aside from the rest of the hospital and a "leaderless" ward system was set up which was designed to display neurosis in the individual, primarily not for the patient and the medical staff, but as a problem for the whole group, in this instance the ward, which was then dealt with by discussions at the morning ward meetings. It was a very radical approach and was applied in a manner that proved too radical for the rest of the hospital. The problem of bed-wetting, for instance, was not left to be coped with in the secretive, orthodox way by the nursing staff, which increased the soldiers' sense of disgrace and inadequacy, but as a problem for the whole ward that had to be discussed openly at the ward meetings. There was, therefore, a minimum of nursing staff and aides. Bion and Rickman participated as observers.

The prime reason for terminating the experiment lay in the anxiety of the "authorities" that such a radical approach would undermine discipline, and the last straw came when the dining-hall was left in a state of disorder following a film show and the floor was left strewn with newspapers and used contraceptives. Bion and Rickman were shortly afterwards posted to the War Office to set up the procedure at the War Office Selection Boards for potential officers where, among other things, they were assessed on their conduct as observed in small leaderless groups, tackling various problems of strategy!

Late in 1944, Rickman was to revisit Northfield at the time of the second experiment of Foulkes. His visit proved highly stimulating and it was not until then that Foulkes became fully aware of the details of the first experiment.

It was typical of Foulkes's whole philosophy that he approached the problem in an entirely different and more circumspect manner in what he called Phase A of the second Northfield experiment. This involved the very modest beginning in 1943 of enlisting the enthusiasm and support of the then Commanding Officer, Lt Colonel Rosie, a self-effacing, highly intelligent Scot, to introduce small-group weekly meetings with certain of the patients from his own ward, which consisted of seventy to eighty patients.

During this phase, he was observing a principle he had already thought out: to regard the total situation, in this instance the whole hospital, as his frame of reference, and this included all the hospital staff, not only the converted, but those who were remote and stood in some kind of opposition and who made, by the way, an indispensable contribution, too, quite apart from the fact that people were, of course, not divided into two factions of "pros" and "cons" like black and white sheep. They had an overall basis of common ground and enthusiastic devotion in their duties inside the hospital as a whole—as it should be in a good group (1948).

Subsequently in my career, I had occasion to regret that I did not follow this principle more fully. Where I had done so at St George's Hospital, the group work reached fruition, but where I failed to do so at Halliwick, the project eventually failed.

His philosophy was to locate the foreground figures against the background as being distinct but essentially related, and to apply the therapeutic lever where so ever it seemed appropriate. I am convinced that it was this dialectic duality between relationship and context that constituted the basis for his success. I do not think that this can be overemphasised, and is only too often understated. What then happened were five major advances.

First, by seeing all his patients on his ward in groups of eight or ten, he was able to observe each soldier more frequently, which saved repetition and therefore time: in other words, all sorts of advantages in matters of expediency.

Second, the regressive tendency activated by individual interviews, which was particularly undermining to morale, was avoided or reduced to a minimum.

Third, therefore, it became apparent that the subtle but vital phenomenon of morale, involving the whole ward, was promoted, which, under those circumstances, was synonymous with improvement. It had a totalising, as distinct from a fragmenting and isolating, effect, and there was less evidence of unwilling soldiers challenging discipline on grounds of health.

Fourth, not only did this procedure have time-saving advantages, but the individual soldiers did qualitatively better than those treated along orthodox individual lines. In particular, not only was the method more successful therapeutically speaking, but it proved strikingly superior in finer diagnostic and prognostic factors.

Fifth, the rest of the hospital became interested and many colleagues, mostly the younger ones, from other wards became more involved and, therefore, more open and responsive to training. It was during the relatively muted stage of Phase A that I first met Foulkes, and it was not till after the BLA campaign was over that I witnessed Phase B, when the whole ward as a community was conducted on small-group lines and which distinguished Phase B from A. Again, it had started off along very modest lines when Foulkes had been given orders to take over a particularly demoralised ward where the psychiatrist had been taken ill and of which the divisional officer had said, "It is in a dreadful condition and must be taken by storm and I have nobody else to do it."

What Foulkes decided was to approach the ward as a group, and the first thing he did was to wander around it to assess the atmosphere by talking to various patients. He realised that handling a group of this sort entailed a painstaking attention to detail. He established a nucleus of co-operative patients, which he formed into a group. He initiated meetings with the nursing staff and encouraged them to participate and to take social histories. Soon, the patients began to experience the value of this interest and he was able to apply a measure of discipline by posting one of the more difficult customers back to his unit. Of this ward experience he wrote,

> I believe I am right in saying that already, after six weeks or so, this ward was the best ward in the hospital, it did not matter in what terms this was measured, whether in general morale, behaviour and bearing in the hospital, regular participation in activities, occupational or social or in disciplinary matters such as absenteeism or in terms of

psychiatric improvement. It is however very interesting that all these items go up and down together. (Foulkes, 1948, p. 109)

Phase B had become organised by the end of 1944, when the Second Front had become an established fact, and all the wards were now being conducted along group lines.

A military staff had been selected who had acquired positive understanding of the psychiatric point of view from experiences with the War Office Selection Boards (WOSB), and in particular of a group psychological orientation. This enabled all those involved—military staff, psychiatrists, and patients—to face the tasks of the hospital as a common concern and the invidious division within the hospital between "Medical Wing" in hospital blues and "Training Wing" in khaki had been judiciously dropped.

By the time I returned to Northfield over a year later, in July 1945, the BLA campaign had ended, VE-Day was over, and Phase B2 was in full swing—"the epilogue of the Northfield Experiment" (so I was not able to see any of Phase B1). I shall never forget the change that had taken place in the meantime. If anything was inscribed on Michael's heart, it must surely have been Northfield Phase B2, when the full impact of his genius made itself felt and had blossomed into fruition. The atmosphere of the hospital was entirely transformed. The enthusiasm that I had seen contained in his personality on the former occasion had now flowered and had spread throughout the whole hospital.

I do not suppose Foulkes ever again reached the same level of intense creative excitement. Nor do I suppose for a moment that it had that much to do with the convening of small analytic groups in a hospital setting. On the contrary, it was more out of the application of what he called "group-analytic principles" to an entire context that, in this instance, resulted in the "large-scale transformation of a whole hospital". This represented the first occasion in which this approach had been attempted and successfully implemented. Eventually, the whole hospital was understood to be a therapeutic group or community, "the first prototype of its kind", which became better known, in a term coined by Tom Main, as a therapeutic community.

Foulkes' capacity to make contact with others was based on this appreciation of the totality of the hospital. He wrote,

It had been a very significant experience for all those who participated in it. Those who did I am sure will agree that the changes which went on in both patients and staff alike were nothing short of revolutionary. From morning to night and from night to morning everything which was seen as relevant was used in the service of a true and quite radical form of therapy. (Foulkes, 1964, p. 207)

But Phase B2, like all Foulkes' undertakings, had had very modest beginnings.

The war was now over and a certain air of apathy had descended upon both staff and patients. The hospital life had become stale and incoherent, the activity side somewhat departmental and institutionalised. What was to be done? I had the good luck, on my own request, to be transferred to the activity department. It became quite clear that levers had to be used to bring about an effect on the hospital spirit as a whole. *The situation suggested the remedy.* Groups had to be formed whose task was directly related to the hospital itself, and who, from their function, were forced into contact and co-operation with others. In principle, as well as in detail, this new approach opened fascinating vistas; one had to find one's way into the heart of groups, or remnants of them, and bring them to life again. Their influence was felt within a week or two throughout the whole hospital, from the Commanding Officer to the last patient, orderly, or office girl. New life blossomed from the ruins. These experiences were among the most interesting I have ever had.

The following quotation is from a paper Foulkes read to the British Psychoanalytic Society in 1945. What he wrote about the same experience thirty years later in 1975 is confirmatory of that statement:

This was an experience which occupied me for day and night for about three years. I hope it will serve as an illustration of principles which have proved of value in psychiatric and other hospitals, as well as in prisons, industry and other institutions of all sorts, especially also educational ones. Of still greater importance are the methods and principles as they grew from the far more subtle observations in small groups, based ultimately on group psychotherapy inspired by the psychoanalytic approach. It is not too much to say that these new methods and principles will increasingly transform the whole of social life, at least in the West. Given good leadership such an objective is realistic as we showed experimentally at Northfield Military Neurosis Centre during World War II. The day will come when whole communities and nations will deal with their affairs in this way. (Foulkes, 1975, p. 5)

At Northfield, Foulkes' philosophy was to allot to the social side of man the same importance as his instinctual nature:

The conviction that man's neuroses and their treatment change their form decisively in accordance with the community in which they arise is fundamental for a group approach. This was experimentally confirmed at Northfield. In psychotherapeutic observations, both in the individual and group situations, I could observe how the patients' minds, concerns, attitudes, and even symptoms changed according to the dynamics of the hospital as a whole.

The large-scale transformation of the hospital developed out of the idea of letting it grow into a self-responsible, self-governing community. No effort was spared to sense the patients' needs to unearth their spontaneously felt desires and urges, to create opportunities for all conceivable activities, whether for work, artistic interest, sports, or entertainments in and outside the confines of the hospital. ... The importance of all this from a therapeutic point of view was that the patient was at every step brought face to face with a social situation; thus, the relationship of the therapeutic group in the narrow sense towards the hospital changed, the smaller unit becoming more definitely orientated towards the larger community of the hospital. The exact way in which the small group changed and re-circulated itself towards the new conditions in the hospital was one of the most interesting points to observe. This showed how the individual person's mind is conditioned by the community in which it exists. Groups were confronted with each other. Many patients improved so much under this management that not only individual treatment but even psychotherapeutic group sessions tended to dry up and become subsidiary to the work project, ward activities, or social activities of the hospital. The effect of all these on the psychiatrists' groups was very interesting, too.

In 1964, Foulkes was to write, somewhat sadly it would seem,

It happens that much of my earlier experiences and experiments were conducted under military conditions, in conjunction with the introduction of group psychotherapy into the psychiatric services of the British Army. What had been a cooperative effort during the War lost its unity afterwards. (Foulkes, 1964, p. 185)

Certainly, subsequently in my own career, I was only to experience anything like the same excitement of Phase B2 at Halliwick in its heyday sometimes, and at the social club at St George's and a large group at the Institute of Group Analysis that met weekly for a year.

What, then, are these group-analytic principles that, in being applied to a hospital context, had such enormous repercussions? At the time, it was not possible to grasp the full implications of these events, though I have little doubt that, from many things Foulkes said, he himself had a very clear visionary realisation.

Since those days in which the environment had forced itself upon us in the form of warfare, I think we have lost ground. We have become more academic, less empirical, superficially more established, but less rooted, less attuned to certain social realities, less political and less cultural in the best sense of being citizens, less prepared to recognise that, though the war is over, the dispute for this more dynamic and comprehensive approach is still going on, but in a very muted form; the apathy that descended on Northfield at the end of the war in Europe has continued. Basically, the contribution of Foulkes and Northfield was the handling of a new dimension; the social, the cultural, and the political in relationship to neurosis. Neurosis, in isolation, is a relatively uninteresting condition and it is only when its true nature in relationship to context is "located" that its meaningfulness begins to be revealed, when meaning itself becomes located as the experience of individual and context, establishing a relationship with each other. This was the significance of Northfield. This was what the excitement was about, but this was only a beginning!

I realise today that what I had witnessed there was a man vitalised by the discovery of this crucial issue, of the link between the deepest "vertical" levels of the intrapersonal psychoanalytic with its "horizontal" transpersonal social context.

His description of group-analytic psychotherapy in his last book in 1975 was that

> group-analytic psychotherapy is a method of group psychotherapy initiated by myself from 1940 onwards in private psychiatric practice and out-patients clinics. It grew out of, and is inspired by, my experience as a psychoanalyst, but also it is *not* a psychoanalysis of individuals in a group. Nor is it the psychological treatment of a group by a psychoanalyst. It is a form of psychotherapy *by* the group *of the* group, including its conductor. Hence the name 'Group Analytic Psychotherapy'. (Foulkes, 1975, p. 3)

From this description follow the four group-analytic principles, which he was to describe as applicable "to all forms of human groups even if they are not primarily therapeutic". These principles are:

1. The total situation is the frame of reference for all operations and for the interpretation and understanding of all observable events. Situation, in this connection, comprises all the objective reality circumstances and the rules, explicit or implicit, observed in the encounter. (I myself would see this as the contextual structure of the group.)

2. All persons involved in the enterprise, institution, or project must be brought together and meet regularly for full and frank discussion and interchange of information and viewpoints. Maximal mutual awareness and communication is the aim, shared as far as possible by all concerned and therefore enabling the whole group to take an active part in their enterprises. Given good leadership, such an objective is realistic, as was shown experimentally at Northfield. (I myself would see this as the relationship and the relating dimension, the negotiating processes, the dialogue, which takes place within the context.)

The other two principles concern the leaders using their abilities, in the best interest of the group, "the group's servant and follower", and the exploration of the situation not as it *appears* to be but for what it really is. Both of these would seem to follow upon the first two principles and are, therefore, secondary and concern the psychoanalytic aspect of the group. The implication of these principles is simply that they comprise two distinct categories of an inseparable duality, two sides of the same coin negotiating with each other. Never for an instant is it feasible for one to become superimposed upon the other. In gestalt terms, the background is represented by the context of the group, and the figure by the relating processes within the group; both are in antithetical interaction with each other.

In brief, what I am saying is that Foulkes at Northfield was legitimately excited not by the application of *psychoanalytic* principles to a whole hospital, but by the application of small-group principles that involved the large-scale transformation of that hospital. Theoretically, it is crucial to make this distinction, since it has considerable implications for the future development of group analysis. This is likely to involve not so much community, but a specified large group *per se* applying group-analytic principles to a large-group setting. In no other setting is the inseparable duality of relationship and context made so glaringly obvious. These two categories are distinct and constitute a consistent binary system, which can, for instance, be in complete opposition in a dialectic process across a transitional boundary zone.

The psychoanalyst is a transitional object; the group, on the other hand, provides a transitional context. In analysis, the relationship is displayed in the form of the transference. In groups, particularly large groups, a duality has arisen in which the context is also made clear and this should be clearly differentiated. I have called it *transposition* since it deserves a name. Freud made the astounding comment that "hypnosis is a group of two". Only by telescoping the relationship (of two) with the context (of a group) could he have arrived at this conclusion, and only because most groups are at a rudimentary stage of relative mindlessness can the patient succumb to the mindless and ego-less state of hypnosis.

What Foulkes did was to become a liaison officer between various groups, for example, reflective and activity, moving from "armchair" to "open-air" psychotherapy and fashioning a small "co-ordination group" to do likewise.

What he did *not* achieve was the next step of putting the small groups into a direct, primary, face-to-face situation with each other. Rather like a shaman, he himself took on the function of the large reflective group; the mode of communication was indirect, through the other small-group activities, via himself as distinct from a direct dialogue. As he described it (1975), "To interpret, therefore, is to transfer or to translate from one context to another". What still remains to be clarified is the nature of these contexts. In 1942, he was describing group therapy as an altogether desirable contribution to people's education as responsible citizens. In his chapter in *The Large Group*, in 1975, he was still writing that the group is perhaps the first adequate practicable approach to the key problem of our time, the strained relationship between the individual and the community. It is now up to us to take that step, *viz.*, the more direct application of principles that Foulkes culled from small-group psychotherapy to larger settings, where the emphasis is less upon psychotherapy and more upon delicate civilising processes.

References

De Maré, P. (1983). Michael Foulkes and the Northfield experiment. In: M. Pines (Ed.), *The Evolution of Group Analysis* (pp. 218–231). London: International Library of Group Psychotherapy and Group Process: Routledge & Kegan Paul.

Foulkes, S. H. (1948). *Introduction to Group-Analytic Psychotherapy: Studies in the Social Integration of Individuals and Groups.* London: Maresfield Reprints, Karnac, 1983.

Foulkes, S. H. (1964). *Therapeutic Group Analysis.* London: Allen & Unwin.

Foulkes, S. H. (1975). *Group Analytic Psychotherapy, Method and Principles.* New York: Gordon & Breach Science Publishers.

CHAPTER THREE

Major Bion*

Patrick de Maré

B oth Bion and Foulkes started off believing that the larger group context, in this instance manifesting itself as a nation in a state of war, was an essential dimension in the handling of neurosis. For Bion, matters of morale, *esprit de corps*, discipline, punishment, and communal responsibility were prime considerations, and led him to raise serious doubts about the suitability of a hospital milieu for psychotherapy; he suggested the name "training unit" or "training wing" instead. He wrote,

> the neurotic is commonly regarded as being self-centred and averse to cooperative endeavours; but perhaps this is because he is seldom put in an environment in which *every* member is on the same footing as regards interpersonal relationships. (Bion, 1961, pp. 24–25)

Then follows his cryptic comment: "The experiment was interrupted by the posting of personnel, so I cannot give clinical or statistical results" (ibid., p. 25).

---

*Previously published in 1985 in: M. Pines (Ed.), *Bion and Group Psychotherapy* (pp. 108–113). London: International Library of Group & Group Process: Routledge & Kegan Paul.

In all, the first Northfield experiment conducted by Majors John Rickman and Wilfred Bion lasted six weeks.

Later, Lt Colonel Tom Main was to remark that the hospital machine unfortunately produced a "desocializing effect", and he described how the traditional hospital milieu produced a refugee culture that was not appropriate for the treatment of war casualties since it produced a passivity and depending atmosphere of "patients grateful to the presiding psychiatrist, himself educated to play a grandiose role among the sick". Main (1946) suggested the term that was more appropriate, which was "therapeutic community".

The crucial issue that was discussed by Rickman, Bion, Foulkes, and Main was the link between the deepest "vertical", intrapersonal axis with the transpersonal "horizontal" of the social and cultural context.

Following the ending of hostilities, a slowing-down of this dynamic approach to large group issues developed; this occasioned Foulkes to write, in 1964,

> It happens that much of my earlier experiences and experiments were conducted under military conditions, in conjunction with the intro-duction of group psychotherapy into the psychiatric services of the British Army. What has been a cooperative effort during the war lost its unity afterwards. (Foulkes, 1964, p. 185)

This first flush of enthusiasm lost its initial momentum as a result partly, perhaps, of Rickman's untimely death, and partly because of Bion's gradual withdrawal from the group field altogether. The groups conducted at the Tavistock Clinic fell dramatically from about forty a week to, at one point, only five, and there was a gradual tilting towards the psychoanalytic model from the social therapy of the two Northfield experiments towards an increasing emphasis on individual psychodynamics.

An example of the original enthusiasm occurred in 1945, when a commission of American psychiatrists, who made a three-thousand-mile tour to investigate the psychiatric resources of the Army Medical Services in the European theatre, eventually stayed for a period of several weeks as guests of the British War Office. Karl Menninger wrote in 1946 in the *Bulletin of the Menninger Clinic,*

> All the members of the commission fell in love with England and its people. One of the things that impressed us most was the skillful use

of the principle of group psychology ... which carried the application of these principles much further than is common in American psychiatric practice ... It is not as yet the method of preference in the leading psychiatric hospitals of America whereas it actually is in England. (Menninger, 1946, p. 65)

The insistence of Bion was that the situation had to be a real-life situation, and this he carried out subsequently in the technique he and Rickman evolved in the War Office Selection Boards, wherein potential officers were tested, not in a free-for-all competition with other candidates, but as members of a group of eight or nine people with some such programme as building a bridge. These were called "Leaderless Group tests".

Referring to the first Northfield experiment, Bion wrote in "The Leaderless Group project", in the same *Bulletin*,

The flight from neurotic disorder had to be stopped; as in a regiment, morale has to be raised to a point where the real enemy could be faced.

To this end discussions were carried out with small groups ... As soon as a sufficient number of patients had in this way been persuaded to face their enemy instead of running away from it, a daily meeting of half-an-hour was arranged for the whole Training Wing, consisting of between a hundred and two hundred men. These meetings were ostensibly concerned only with the organisation of the activities of the Wing. ...

Thus occupational therapy had been given a new meaning. The therapeutic occupation of the group was the study of its own internal life situation, with a view to laying bare the influence of neurotic behaviour introducing frustration, waste of energy and unhappiness in the group ...

The therapeutic occupation had to be hard thinking and not the abreaction of moral indignation. (Bion, 1946, pp. 77–81)

In describing the psychiatrist's problem in stopping a "rout", he wrote, "Outside Nazi Germany psychiatrists are not likely to be shot for doing their job, though of course they may be removed from their posts" (ibid.).

Bion's attitude towards the large meeting was more radical than the subsequent handling of Foulkes in the Second Northfield experiment. Foulkes was more gradualistic in his approach. Bion saw the large meeting of 100–200 people as the main trunk of the tree that could explore the tensions of the smaller activity groups, once he could persuade them to meet, which he arranged, partly by persuasion through small group meetings of chosen members, and partly by simply issuing an order to a parade that would be held every day at 12:10 p.m. for making announcements and conducting other business of the Training Wing. The result of this radical approach was that it produced a cultural clash with the hospital military authorities. The fear that Rickman's and Bion's approach would lead to anarchy and chaos occasioned War Office officials to pay a lightning visit at night. The chaos in the hospital cinema hall, with newspapers and condom strewn floors, resulted in the immediate termination of the project. Majors Rickman and Bion were posted, and set up War Office Selection Boards elsewhere.

Foulkes, in contrast to this, developed the small group meetings with official approval from the Commanding Officer, which took a period of at least a year to prepare. There was then a gradual viewing of the large groups in the form of ward groups of from thirty to eighty men. But he was insistent that

> More is needed, however. The patient needs insight . . . Therein lies the limitedness of a large meeting of thirty to eighty men; the patient's reactions cannot be brought to light, voiced, described, realised or brought home to him by others. For this the more intimate setting is essential. Seven or eight people at a time have proved a good number. They meet regularly from once to three times a week for a set period of one to one-and-a-half hours. (Foulkes, 1964, p. 206)

I personally helped Rickman and Bion to pack. Clearly, Bion was put out by these events. Rickman, on the other hand, merely exclaimed, unrepentantly and unperturbedly, "'Pon my soul!", in the high-pitched tone he sometimes adopted in mock surprise.

I was fortunate in having witnessed both the first Northfield experiment of Rickman and Bion, and also in having co-operated with Foulkes in the second experiment. I have already described these experiences with Foulkes in "Michael Foulkes and the Northfield experiment" (1983). I was first posted to Northfield Hospital in December 1942, having been a Medical Officer attached to a Battle School at Hay Tor in Dartmoor, a most bleak setting, in the late

Autumn of 1942. It was with some relief that I found myself, on the grounds that I had had a year's psychoanalysis and had worked for eleven months at Shenley, and had taken the first part of the DPM, posted as a Trainee Psychiatrist to a three-month course held at Northfield, Birmingham, conducted by Major Rickman. The course was arranged as a series of lectures and seminar meetings. There were altogether ten trainees, of whom five were British, four were American, and one was Polish.

After a week or two, Rickman was joined by his colleague, Wilfred Bion. They were both psychoanalysts, and at that time spoke frequently of the findings of Melanie Klein, which Rickman compared to the acceptance and tolerance of "lumps in the porridge", referring to "good" and "bad" objects. They, like Foulkes, had both seen service in the First World War: Foulkes in the German army, Rickman as an ambulance driver in a Quaker unit (he was a conscientious objector) in Russia, and Bion as a very young officer in the Tank Corps.

The seminars conducted by Rickman were extremely thoughtful and lively. He was much the older man—large, grey haired, bright-eyed, moustached, balding, bespectacled, with sensuous lips, continually smoking a pipe, with a gentle caustic manner, soft-voiced. Everything and everybody seemed to provoke an attitude of a first encounter, with a very slight sense in him of wonder and surprise. He continually referred to the findings and happenings of Freud and of his earlier followers. At the very first meeting of our seminar, he announced in soothing terms that this course was to give us all the opportunity to have a breather, "as if we were at a university", and to take a look at psychiatry in wartime. Coming from a Battle School at the height of the uncertainties of the war, this attitude was enormously consoling and did indeed enable us all to do some hard thinking rather than become paralysed by anxiety.

Bion, on the other hand, was a good deal younger, a Boswell to Rickman's Johnson. He, too, was a massive man, balding with a thick black moustache, high-coloured cheeks, thick-lensed gold-rimmed spectacles, smoking a large Sherlock Holmes pipe. He looked very much the officer of the "old school", and, indeed, came from an upper-class Edwardian background with British Raj connections. He was an extremely shy man, which was belied by his imposing presence. He rarely spoke, and when he did so it would always be in the form of cryptic comments. In the seminars, which he conducted separately from Rickman, he would sit in the circle in profound silence, smoking his pipe and occasionally, after someone had vouchsafed a comment, would emit a loud, prolonged sniff, which was somewhat disconcerting, since it was ambiguous. What could it all mean? Indeed, he would only rarely reveal his thoughts, seated ostensibly as an unobserved observer, but always the centre of unvoiced attention. I remember one comment was that "the working class is always in a state of war", and, on another occasion, that a Tank Officer in the previous war had been seen to be wearing a bullet-proof waistcoat under his uniform, which comment was followed by a contemptuous sniff with the inference that the offender was regarded by fellow-officers as a "poor type", clearly not a "good man", terms that were rife at that time. In contrast to this approach, much talk centred on the Gestalt quasi-Marxist approach of Kurt Lewin and Brown. In fact, the Russians at that time were much favoured by many of us, including Rickman and Bion, and Stalin was referred to as "Uncle Joe". This was shortly after the retreat by the Germans from Stalingrad, the first sign of a breakthrough for the Allies.

The overall impression of those fraught three months was an unforgettable atmosphere of stimulation, thoughtfulness, and interest. Thank you, John Rickman, thank you, Wilfred Bion! I shall never forget you, and to this day I continue to miss you both. The lively meetings were the forerunner to much that subsequently evolved and that was intensively followed up at the Tavistock, at the Cassel, at the Maudsley, at St George's Hospital, above all by Michael Foulkes at the Group Analytic Society, Institute and Practice. Of the four, Foulkes was the least "elitist". Perhaps this accounts for his work having flourished more, even though, at present, the writings of Bion seem to have become more widely published. In a nutshell, it can be said that Bion was more aware of large group and cultural forces than Foulkes, but Foulkes was more radical in seeing the small group as taking on its own therapy, rather than Bion's approach, which continued to recommend ambiguously that the conductor is essentially a work-group leader. Perhaps, if Rickman and Bion's large group project had not been so summarily terminated, history might have taken a very different course. Certainly, in Bion's book, *Experiences in Groups* (1961), one gains the impression that he often handled small groups as if they were large. To my knowledge, neither he nor Rickman ever again attempted a large-group approach.

References

Bion, W. R. (1946). The Leaderless Group project. *Bulletin of the Menninger Clinic, 10*(3): 77–81.

Bion, W. R. (1961). *Experiences in Groups*. London: Tavistock.

De Maré, P. (1983). Michael Foulkes and the Northfield experiment. In: M. Pines (Ed.), *The Evolution of Group Analysis* (pp. 218–230). London: Routledge & Kegan Paul.

Foulkes, S. H. (1948). *Introduction to Group-Analytic Psychotherapy*. London: Heinemann.

Foulkes, S. H. (1964). *Therapeutic Group Analysis*. London: Allen & Unwin.

Main, T. F. (1946). The hospital as a therapeutic institution. *Bulletin of the Menninger Clinic, 10*(3): 66–70.

Menninger, K. A. (1946). Foreword. *Bulletin of the Menninger Clinic, 10*(3): 65.

CHAPTER FOUR

Non-transference elements in group analytic psychotherapy*

Patrick de Maré

In *Group Psychology and The Analysis of the Ego* (1921c), Freud wrote that "from the first there were two kinds of psychology, that of the individual members of the group, and that of the father, chief or leader" (Freud, 1921c, p. 71).

He pointed out in the chapter headed "A differentiating grade in the ego" that in the group setting, the individual gives up his ego ideal and substitutes for it the group ideal as embodied in the leader.

> The libidinal structure of the group leads back to the distinction between the ego and the ego ideal and to the double kind of tie which this makes possible – identification and the substitution of the object for the ego ideal. (Ibid., p. 79)

He made a comparison between hypnosis, being in love, and the group psychology: he described hypnosis as a group of two.

He put it that a primary group "is a number of individuals who have substituted one and the same object for the ego ideal and have consequently identified themselves with one another in their ego" (ibid., p. 61).

In other words, the repressive agent, namely the superego, becomes projected into the conductor *in a group setting*—and a corresponding intrapsychic change occurs within the individual, *viz.* a relatively less repressed ego structure.

Group therapy began at the point where Freud left off. Freud's philosophical background was based on the Cartesian dichotomy of the pure cogito, soul, spirit, or *mind* (in this instance the psychoanalyst) observing *matter* (the patient); two totally distinct substances. (It is worth recalling, however, that Descartes (1996) did concede language as providing evidence of thought.)

The "first scientific revolution" of Descartes and Newton liberated physics from the dead hand of the scholastics, from anthropomorphism, but it took three centuries before the intangible data of the submicroscopic world, of psychology and sociology, could be accommodated by a new model in the philosophy of science and that has been nicknamed the second scientific revolution.

Freud had to rely on the then current formulations in physics and the science of philosophy at the beginning of the century, of the conservation of energy, of the intrapsychic world in isolation, of linear, unidirectional, and progressive cause–effect relations, of psychic energy, and economy.

Lewin (1936), with the new models of quantum physics' electromagnetic field theory, where relationship and organisation rather than energy and matter played a primary role, to draw from, studied the intersubjective field. Around about 1939, he coined the terms group dynamics, systems in tension, and field theory.

With the advent of Wiener's and Shannon's cybernetics and information theory after the Second World War, the shift from the transference of energy to that of information was finally established. With the discovery of feedback, of goal-directed behaviour in machines (e.g., the thermostat), the age-long epistemological controversy between determinism and teleology or vitalism (until then excluded from science) shows signs of reconciliation. The crucial distinction between the psychodynamic (e.g., psychoanalytic) model, on the one hand, and the interdependence and interaction of individual organism and the environment on the other, has been to some extent bridged by information and communication theory. Don Jackson, in *Pragmatics of Human Communication* (Watzlawick, Bavelas, & Jackson, 1967), gives as an example the man who kicks a pebble; the latter will be displaced according to the amount of energy transferred: on the other hand, kicking a dog might result in a bite, when it is information rather than energy that is transferred. This is essentially the difference between Freudian psychodynamics and the theory of communication as explanatory principles of human behaviour, and which is so striking a feature of group dynamics.

The cybernetic model, with its reflexive nature of interaction, provides us with a comparative study of automatic control systems, or organisation, of communication and information-storage, whether of the nervous system and brain or of mechanical electrical devices. It involves the self-checking, correcting, regulating system of feedback circuits, of the loop system of internal dependencies. Gregory Bateson (1979) has put it: "we don't know tuppence about the total network system". Feedback can be "negative", preserving a steady state of homoeostasis maintaining the stability of relationships, or it can be positive, leading to change and loss of stability—in both cases, part of a system's output is reintroduced back into the system as information about its output.

Foulkes' ideas from the beginning were based on the concept that all psychodynamics are originally multi-personal, at the very least two-personal, and refer ultimately to the group (tribe, family, community, species) and are primarily group phenomena. Psychodynamics are not only interpersonal but transpersonal phenomena and go to the very roots of any approach to group psychology. It requires a fundamental turn of mind for which the undergoing of group analytic treatment is perhaps the best preparation.

> *The attitude is psycho-analytical but the method and technique is new. The background of consideration is the mental matrix of the group as a whole, inside which all intrapsychic processes interact.* This has a profound significance for psycho-analytic concepts ... the observations now possible in this group analytic situation give rise to new insights and theoretical concepts. The new situation leads to new concepts. (Foulkes, 1964, preface)

He calls it a multi-personal, supraindividual field.

Foulkes, inspired by Trigant Burrow in the first place, put the group in the centre of his orientation. "That was and remains his great merit", he said, speaking of Burrow.

Group psychotherapy, Foulkes stated (1964), can be practised with or without an analytic orientation; he himself is only concerned with the latter.

In his early article of 1942, he states that the "group has, however, some specific therapeutic factors" (Foulkes, 1964, p. 33), of which he singles out (i) the sharing, socialising effect, (ii) the mirror reaction, (iii) the activating of the collective unconscious, the stimulating effect of the group situation, (iv) the exchange and information elements, (v) the form that communication took, namely that of group association modelled on free association, of free floating discussion developed to its full extent. Essentially, these group specific features, which he elaborated upon later, concern activation, communication, and socialisation, of which socialisation is specific to the group situation.

> This proves large enough (7 or 8 patients and the therapist) to observe psychological reactions in their social context. The group is also large enough to be representative of its community, yet it is intimate enough to trace the ramifications of these reactions in the individual member and to explore their roots inside the individual. (Ibid., p. 55)

The group situation, in other words, introduces new features of its own which are not present in the individual situation between one therapist and one patient. He said, *"This is true though the majority of group therapists are not aware of it at the present time"* (ibid., p. 38). He sees the conductor's function as catalytic—as a participant observer—"the therapist is put in the position of a primordial leader image".

"He can actually be said to be a father figure and it is all too easy to interpret his position really as that of a father, a mother, and see the group as representing a family. *This is not my impression"* (ibid., p. 59). "Group psychology must develop its own concepts in its own right and not borrow them from individual psychology. The group is older than the individual" (ibid., p. 60).

Quoting Freud, "we must conclude that the psychology of the group is the oldest human psychology".

The group, Foulkes suggests, reanimates the archaic inheritance, and it is the impetus of this reanimation which is harnessed for therapeutic purpose in group therapy.

The passing episodes of leadership (as described by Fritz Redl) in a continuous flow with a gradual decrescendo move from his authoritarian position, are gradually replaced by reliance on the strength of the group itself, which Foulkes later developed in his theory of the group matrix. Two moves are taking place; a decrescendo away from authoritarianism and a crescendo towards socialisation.

If he thinks, for instance, in terms of transference of the family group containing father, mother, and siblings, of projection, identification, repression, resistance, reaction formation, fixation, and so on, merely in the way these appear in the individual situation, he will find all these, to be sure, in operation, but he will not learn much that is new. If he thinks, however, of the group situation that he has in front of him, he will find a wealth of new observations, as regards the dynamics of the group, and, indeed, new light will be thrown upon the mechanisms operating in individual psychoanalysis.

The paramount need here is to create a scientific view of group psychodynamics in a language that is commonly understood . . . the group situation becomes the natural meeting ground of the biologist, anthropologist, sociologist, and psychoanalyst.

We do not think that there are any such factors that may not appear in some guise in other types of group. What distinguishes our analytic groups is not the presence of certain unique factors, but the particular combination of the several factors that we have already enumerated and the way in which they are used.

There is the free-floating verbal communication carried to an extreme point; there is the maximum reduction of censorship of personal and interpersonal feelings; there is the attitude of the conductor, who not only actively cultivates and maintains the group atmosphere and the active participation of members, but also allows himself to become a transference figure in the psychoanalytic sense and accepts the changing roles which the group assign him; there is the emphasis on the unconscious repressed of psychoanalysis, and on the interpersonal and social unconscious in the group-analytic sense; there is analysis and interpretation of the material produced by the group.

It is the concerted application of all these elements in a judiciously selected interplay that makes a situation therapeutic. The *psychoanalytic situation is known in such a capacity as a "transference situation"*. Some writers (e.g., Ezriel) declare the group therapeutic situation to be not more and not less than a transference situation in a group setting. As we have pointed out in the first chapter, we feel it *important to distinguish between transference and non-transference elements*, both being part of the therapeutic process. We propose, therefore, to signify those properties of the (psycho-) therapeutic situation that make it essentially therapeutic by the symbol "T". We can then formulate that some authors consider "T" as identical with "transference"

(T = t), whereas the present authors consider that a "T" situation must allow for the dynamic confrontation of the patient with both the transference (t) and non-transference (x = current relationships "here-and-now", etc.) aspects of his reactions (T = t + x).

In the T situation, past and present must meet. The past, which was unconscious, repressed, or never experienced in such form as could be recalled except through repetition behaviour, is accepted as present in the T situation. In the same process, however, the real present (the current situation, the immediate context, the "here-and-now") must be represented as well for the analytic therapeutic process to operate.

In connexion with this, it is one of the relevant conditions that the participants in a group-analytic group are strangers except for their contact within the group. The very personal and real emotions and attitudes between members thus remain inside the T situation, and are prevented from spilling over into ordinary life.

Foulkes, at some point, states that but for certain group features referring in particular to the phenomenon he calls location, he might very well not have taken up his interest in group therapy at all.

The transference situation in the group is on a much broader front. It is horizontal rather than vertical. The individual patients' transference relationship to the conductor or to any other member of the group cannot develop to anything like the same extent as in psychoanalysis and cannot always be analysed vertically to anything like the same degree.

> For the study of this wider field, of the location and constellation of his disturbance with its complex network of human relationship the group situation provides an indispensible means of bringing essential patterns into focus. Within the group analytic situation we have, instead of the individual transference relationship between patient and therapist, a whole spectrum of relationship in active operation before our eyes. (Foulkes & Anthony, 1965, p. 50)

He points out that, while in psychoanalysis the interpretations are made by the analyst, *in the group, all members participate actively*. It is a multi-personal situation in which regression, including the strictly psychoanalytic phenomenon of transference, is not encouraged. The full analysis of individual transference is not possible and the transference neurosis is not fully promoted and established. While, in psychoanalysis, there is verbal analysis with emphasis upon insight and on contact between past and present (in group analysis the emphasis is upon action and *experience*), ego training is an active and a corrective experience, not by the analyst, but by the slowly emerging group network, which becomes progressively more complex and sophisticated and affiliative, as distinct from hierarchical.

In brief, the group situation has an immediate and very powerful impact; if you wish to, you can call it a sort of collective archaic transference, which is universal, for it occurs in all groups everywhere and is not confined to neurotics (as transference is said to do in the transference neurosis), nor is it unconscious. In fact, the projecting of the ego ideal on to the conductor or leader results in a lifting of repressive forces within the individual; the content of the personal repressed is not the focus of interest: rather, a profound modification takes place in the superego once it becomes, as it were, the property of the group, which is then translated from a primitive archaic authoritarian institution by communication to a socialising group matrix. Anything that holds up this process of communication, whether intrapersonal, interpersonal, or transpersonal, is treated as it arises. This, therefore, does not exclude transference interpretations, provided this is forming the greater barrier, but the effect of such interpretation might have its repercussions in rendering the group constellation more leader-centred.

Bion put it succinctly in saying, "In the treatment of the individual, neurosis is displayed as a problem of the individual. In the treatment of a group it must be displayed as a problem of the group" (Bion & Rickman, 1943, p. 678).

All approaches can be expressed diagrammatically and located in relationship to each other within a triangular area, depending upon such variables as task, members, orientation of conductor, size of group, etc. The positionings of the various approaches are only approximations, serving as indications or suggestions.

References

Bateson, G. (1979). *Mind and Nature: A Necessary Unity*. New York: E. P. Dutton.

Bion, W. R., & Rickman, J. (1943). Intra-group tensions in therapy: their study as the task of the group. *Lancet, 245*: 678–681.

Descartes, R. (1996). *Discourse on the Method and Meditations on First Philosophy.* New Haven, CT: Yale University Press.

Foulkes, S. H. (1964). *Therapeutic Group Analysis.* London: Allen & Unwin.

Foulkes, S. H., & Anthony, E. J. (1965). *Group Psychotherapy: The Psychoanalytic Approach.* Harmondsworth: Penguin.

Freud, S. (1921c). *Group Psychology and the Analysis of the Ego. S.E., 18*: 67–143. London: Hogarth.

Lewin, K. (1936). *Principles of Topological Psychology,* G. Heider & F. Heider (Trans.). New York: McGraw-Hill.

Watzlawick, P., Bavelas, J. B., & Jackson, D. D. (1967). *Pragmatics of Human Communication: A Study of Interactional Patterns, Pathologies and Paradoxes.* New York: W. W. Norton.

PART II
LARGE GROUPS

"The fateful question for the human species seems to be whether and to what extent their cultural development will succeed in mastering the disturbance of their communal life by the human instinct of aggression and self-destruction."

(Freud, 1930a, p. 154)

"All feeling, whether in a group or elsewhere, is a manifestation of psychic energy. That feeling is a result of instincts, which are themselves very ancient habits. The feelings choose to direct energy in a certain way. Energy is only itself, the stuff of which the universe is made; it lies about the universe in various forms, sometimes active, sometimes passive and dormant. Humanity has discovered ways of channeling it throughout the world and beyond. What it could now attempt is to channel its psychic energy in ways that do not lead to destruction and disintegration within the social world."

(de Maré, 1989, pp. 186–187)

"The only answer to mass violence is mass dialogue."

(Ibid., p. 181)

References

De Maré, P. (1989). The history of large group phenomena in relation to group analytic psychotherapy: the story of the median group. *Group*, 13(3–4): 173–197.

Freud, S. (1930a). *Civilization and Its Discontents. S.E., 21*: 59–145. London: Hogarth.

Introduction to large groups

Lionel Kreeger

M y first contact with Pat was in January 1965, when he inter-
viewed me for the post of Consultant Psychotherapist at
Halliwick Hospital, where he had worked for three years in
addition to his appointment to the Psychiatric Department of St
George's Hospital. I was struck immediately by his warm welcome,
his open generosity in response to me, and his genuine interest in my
work and background. I was delighted when I was appointed to this
position, and later I was granted further sessions as Consultant
Psychiatrist and took over a thirty-bed ward in addition to continuing
the overall work of developing the therapeutic community milieu. Pat
and I worked closely together with ward and community meetings,
and it was in the course of this shared experience that we together
developed our fascination with large groups and their intriguing
dynamics. Concurrently, Pat was instrumental in bringing me into the
Group Analytic Practice in 1967, and kindly allowed me to share his
consulting room.

The years 1972 to 1974 were crucial to our relationship and the
development of our interest and enthusiasm for the large group, both
clinically and in training. In May 1972, the Second European
Symposium of Group Analysis took place in London and as part of

that conference Pat and I introduced a three-hour session of the Large Group. It created much interest and enthusiasm and led to the incorporation of Large Groups into most symposia and workshops thereafter. In January 1973, at the European Workshop in Group Analysis, Pat and I led the daily Large Group, and the late Isobel Jacobs (Jacobs, 1973) reported on all five sessions for *Group Analysis*. She captured brilliantly the unfolding dynamics of the group, the ambivalent relationship between Pat and myself and the threatened battles for leadership. To quote from her report,

> Ambivalence was personified in our two staff members who acknowledged their rivalry for leadership. The fact that they recognized their differences as old ones and that Dr. Kreeger referred calmly to the possibility of conflict breaking out between them provided us with a model for coming to terms with ambivalence. Both agreed that there was a dependent part of the group and until negative feelings had been expressed we could not give expression to positive ones. Each took the group in different directions. Dr. Kreeger saw our proceedings in terms of pre-Oedipal object relations whereas Dr. de Maré expounded his distinction between the hierarchical leader whose interventions bring communication to a full stop, and the spokesman of leading ideas who appears now from one part of the group and then from another. He urged us to brave the terrors of merging with each other without hierarchy in order to release the explosive power of the Large Group. He held out the prospect of freeing the individual from the effect of social blows received in other settings and closed hierarchical systems. The session ended excited and hopeful for the future of the Large Group. (Kreeger, 1975, p. 27)

It was through these experiences of working with Pat that led to my editing *The Large Group* (Kreeger, 1975) containing Pat's chapter "The politics of the large group", which I believe to be one of Pat's most concise and significant of his many writings. I particularly value the statement that, "To apply small group or psychoanalytic models to the large group is like trying to play Ludo on a chessboard" (ibid., p. 146).

When I left Halliwick Hospital in 1973, having become disillusioned and frustrated with the envious and destructive assaults on its therapeutic integrity, I did experience considerable feelings of guilt towards him, but he has never held it against me. Indeed we were able to co-author a book, *An Introduction to Group Treatment in Psychiatry* (de Maré & Kreeger, 1974) over the subsequent year, which, for me, was undoubtedly reparative in intent. It was dedicated to the patients and staff at Halliwick Hospital, so that, with its ultimate closure, it has also become a memorial to the demise of this exciting venture, which had the potential to become the ideal model for other psychodynamically orientated units.

To return to Pat's chapter, "The politics of large groups", in my edited *The Large Group*, it certainly has several references to the concept of Koinonia, but no mention yet of the median group! He referred merely to the two primary structures of small groups of up to twenty people and large groups from twenty upwards. In his 1991 book, *Koinonia* (co-authored with Piper and Thompson), he and his colleagues discuss the large group and its dynamics and then proceed to the definition of the median group and its metastructure. He talks of "kith, kin, and Koinionia", in which a kinship mode of work, which is natural, can, through dialogue with kithship, which is social, create the atmosphere of Koinonia. Koinonia itself refers to the development of impersonal fellowship, a culture of togetherness and amity, transforming the chaos of mindlessness and hate into more human communion. In essence, it is the transformation of hate towards the emergence of gratitude.

I have myself wondered occasionally whether the dynamics of the median group are so different from those of a small, large group, but I respect Pat's own enthusiastic conviction of its uniqueness, a bridge between the small group and the large. I have wondered whether there has been some practical consideration leading to the creation of the concept of the median group because of the difficulties of the organisation of large group meetings compared with the more moderate structural demands of the median group. For example, I conducted the large group of the Qualifying Course at the Institute of Group Analysis, London for many years, in the early days hosting between thirty and forty participants, but, in recent years, for various reasons, numbers have diminished somewhat and the average attendance has dropped to perhaps fifteen to twenty. I have asked myself many times whether there is a significant difference in the dynamics between the two, whether a median group has its own specific integrity beyond that of being a small, large group.

In their book *Koinonia* (de Maré, Piper, & Thompson, 1991), de Maré and his colleagues widen their vision of the large group approach to a micro-culture of society, a watershed between the world and the personal individual experiential mind, which offers the opportunity to humanise both the individual and society concurrently. The process of dialogue constitutes a transformational change from mindlessness to understanding, and thus to meaning. Hate gives way to the emergence of gratitude.

In his contribution to the special issue of *Group Analysis* (Hopper, 2000) honouring Pat, Earl writes of his discussions with Pat on citizenship and the politics of large group processes, his interest in the context of such groups, as in organisations and even society as a whole. Hopper argues that it was really a way of being politically active rather than actually demonstrating in Trafalgar Square.

I end this Introduction with the expression of my own gratitude to, and love for, Pat for the many years of close and creative experiences we have shared. It is most sad that this volume has to be published posthumously, but I was privileged to visit Pat in hospital on the morning of his death and reminded him of the efforts being made to finalise the manuscript. He smiled and whispered, "Lovely."

References

De Maré, P., & Kreeger, L. C. (1974). *Introduction to Group Treatment in Psychiatry*. London: Butterworths.

De Maré, P., Piper, R., & Thompson, S. (1991). *Koinonia*. London: Karnac.

Hopper, E. (2000). From objects and subjects to citizens: group analysis and the study of maturity. *Group Analysis, 33:* 29–34.

Jacobs, I. (1973). Report on the Large Group at the European Workshop on Group Analysis. *Group Analysis, 1*(3): 26–28.

Kreeger, L. C. (Ed.) (1975). *The Large Group, Dynamics and Therapy*. London: Constable [reprinted London: Maresfield, 1994].

CHAPTER FIVE

Large group psychotherapy: a suggested technique*

Patrick de Maré

Preamble

T hat neurosis is a response to a maladjusted society is a relatively old theme. Wilfred Trotter's "Instincts of the herd in peace and war" (1919) compared neurosis to the warning signal of pain. Cody Marsh somewhat earlier (1909) had a Group Therapy Credo, "By the crowd they have been broken; by the crowd shall they be healed" (de Maré, 1975, p. 149).

However, the technique of large group psychotherapy, which would appear to be a self-evident conclusion, continues to meet with the suspicion that was once accorded to psychoanalysis and later to small group psychotherapy, witness the opposition to the Paddington Day Hospital and other therapeutic communities. And, although a good deal has been said about therapeutic communities, the intensive and rigorous application of a large group technique *per se* has not yet been seriously mooted.

The explanation for this might lie in the powerful, chaotic, and unpredictable nature of large group phenomena and in their tendency

*This paper was first published in 1972, in *Group Analysis*, 5: 106–108.

to ideology formation, which would prove politically and economi-cally dicey in many countries today. Simpler and safer, in that case, to remain psychoanalytically based.

Social awareness

Mankind has progressed through various phases, pagan religions, philosophical, scientific, psychological, and is now on the brink of an emerging sociological awareness. It is this sort of socially based insight that might well prove to be psychotherapeutic if practised in a large group setting. In parentheses, it is worth mentioning that the derivation of the word consciousness is "knowing something in oneself with others" (*Shorter Oxford Dictionary*). It would follow that the construct of a group mind, in that case, would be more consistent than that of the individual mind. The unconscious mind is, in that case, the mind that is not shared.

Suggested constitution of a large therapy group

Fifty to a hundred people seated in a circle or a two-tiered circle (which could easily be arranged with the outer circle in chairs and the inner circle on cushions or stools) would be a feasible arrangement. (Incidentally, the amphitheatres of ancient Greece had magnificent acoustics and seated several thousand.) These meetings should be arranged as rigorously and intensively as the psychoanalytic or small group setting, for example, closed daily meetings of 1½ hours' dura-tion over a period of two or more years.

Large group dynamics

The large group plays an antithetically opposite role to that of the small group. While the small group only too readily lends itself to a psychodynamic approach, usually psychoanalytic, the large group manifests characteristically specific group dynamic features. In the former, that of the here and now, manifesting topological phenomena such as projection, splitting, and displacement, transposition rather than transference of total current or past social situations, total cultures and climates, total worlds. In fact, the amplifying and totalising effect of the large group is most striking when emotions sweep like an atmosphere or a breeze throughout the entire group.

While the problem for the member of a small group is how to feel spontaneously, for the large group, it is primarily how to think. Freud recognised something of the sort when he pointed out the dilemma of having to procure for the group (and he referred to large groups) precisely those features which were characteristic of the individual, and which are extinguished in him by the formation of the group. While the problem for the individual and for the small group is the intrusion of unconscious factors (Bion has called them basic assumptions), for the large group it is consciousness that is in quandary, or the group's equivalent of consciousness: communication and organisation. The problem for the large rudimentary group is its mindlessness.

Despite the enormous potential of information flow which is at the disposal of the members of the large group, intelligence is only too easily blocked by energy flow; intelligence succumbs to coercion; the loud mouth silences the still small voice of intuition; affiliative communication "on the level" gives way to hierarchical non-communication; leading ideas and trends give way to the pressures and transferences of personality and leadership.

Because of its evident power, the large group's impact on its environment is far more marked than that, for instance, of the small closed group or of psychoanalysis "behind closed doors". Hence, the stringent laws pertaining to large public meetings. Hence, too, the somewhat precarious careers of therapeutic communities to date.

The social matrix is a useful construct because it refers to the ongoing dynamic processes involving the growth of a communicational network. Where this network is still only at a rudimentary stage, panic, rage, splitting, displacement, and projecting are characteristic. Many writers assume that this is characteristic of all large groups always, while, in fact, it is only an early phase. Where chaos was, there shall matrix be, should be the dictum for the large group. Turquet (1975) has read a paper entitled "Threats to identity in the large group. A study in the phenomenology of the individual's experience in groups". This refers to six to eight meetings of 40–60 members.

In fact, given the opportunity to meet, the large group evolves a network sufficiently consistent to contain this split.

Panic and rage are far more likely to occur when the network is still at a tenuous rudimentary stage of development. While panic fragments, rage and hate unite; hate is the motive power to thought processes, to intelligence and intelligibility (as distinct from thought disorder and intellectualisation). In large group therapy, intelligence and communicability and transposition are primary features, as distinct from libido and transference in psychoanalysis.

The hierarchy to end all hierarchies is that of the family. The compulsion to repeat this setting in the large group is enormous. The result is that members in a large group have a tendency to create a structure that is neither realistic nor gratifying. Having colluded [in making the] self-same structure in a caricature form, the members are then faced with the task of reshaping it. The large group, because of its immense plasticity and capacity to change (morphogenesis), offers us an appropriate setting in which to carry this out. Invisible barriers (intrapersonal) are projected as tangible constellations and role-playing relationships (interpersonal and transpersonal), which the members have the opportunity to reconstitute. This differs from the small group setting in being so much more manifest and amplified, so much more palpable. What has to be maintained, if growth and therapy is to occur, is a permeability at the interface between the self-system of the individual and the social system of the large group: both must remain open to the other.

The large group

Report from Dr Andrew Cockburn

In his opening remarks, Lionel Kreeger reminded us of how much interest in large groups is increasing: two areas of particular concern are the use of large groups in the institutional setting, particularly a therapeutic community, and in the course of training schemes. After outlining some of the views of S. H. Foulkes, Maxwell Jones, Edelson and Rafael Springmann, Kreeger spoke of the role of the large group and its possible value in relation to the current trend towards smaller hospital units and the increasing emphasis on community care. Large group organisation might become the only feasible way of attempting to deal with the psychotherapeutic needs of the hospital population. Kreeger expressed the view that:

1. The matrix of a large group may reside in a nucleus of staff members or leaders who, because of the constant fluctuation in the total constitution of the group, thereby contain the history and culture of the group.

2. The question of large groups splitting into sub-groups is seen very much as a defence against the massive paranoid anxieties that might occur in a large group. There is a need for greater awareness of this process, with the corollary that resistance to the realisation of the splits might lead to the tendency for large groups to break up physically into smaller groups in order to function more effectively.

Pat de Maré, following Lionel Kreeger, spoke of the need for some really new thinking and the necessity to get away from the classic psychoanalytic model of transference, particularly in considering the large group, which manifests characteristically specific group dynamic features. For example the horizontal–spatial dimension of the here and now, manifest in phenomena such as projection, splitting, and displacement; the transposition rather than transference of current or past social situations.

References

De Maré, P. (1975). The politics of large groups. In: L. Kreeger (Ed.), The Large Group: Dynamics and Therapy (pp. 145–158). London: Karnac.

Trotter, W. (1919). Instincts of the Herd in Peace and War. London: Fisher Unwin.

Turquet, P. (1975). Threats to identity in the large group. In: L. Kreeger (Ed.), The Large Group: Dynamics and Therapy (pp. 87–144). London: Karnac.

CHAPTER SIX

The politics of large groups*

Patrick de Maré

T o his very fingerprints, each individual is essentially unique. By the same token, society inevitably appears alien to him. This constitutes an ever-present dilemma that can never be finally resolved. But it gives rise to ongoing processes of communication, so that the problem is not so much a matter of authenticity (in any case a value judgement) as one involving the degree to which informational flow can be negotiated. As Jaspers (1963) put it, "Truth is communicability" (rather than, as some would have it, a special preserve of madness).

Levi-Strauss (1949) has suggested that we cannot, though we will, evade the law of exchange, for it is upon exchange that the whole of the cultural structure is built. To enjoy power without sharing it, to separate it from its informational roots, from society and communion, always ends in disaster. Currently, for example, the economic power of bankers bears no relationship to the real wealth and productivity potential of the modern world; as a result, mankind itself is being

---

*This chapter was first published in 1975, in: L. Kreeger (Ed.), *The Large Group* (pp. 145–158). London: Constable (reprinted London: Karnac, 1994). It is reprinted here by permission of Karnac.

treated as a form of pollution, the "population explosion" in the constraining ethos of an effete accountancy system, where money, not wealth, is power. Form has become confused with substance. Generative purpose gives way to futile obsessionalism. Humanity is being gelded by guilt.

The conceptual shift from matter–energy to information flow, previously confused, marks a major breakthrough in the history of science. A parallel shift has taken place in psychosocial thinking—from the psychobiological to the socio-cultural perspective. If we are to survive at all, we can no longer put off the day when the psychological, the politico-economic and the socio-cultural contexts must meet operationally in a unified field. What is imperative is large-group thinking. The World Health Organization, in 1959, naïvely recommends fitting the individual by re-establishing social adequacy and entirely overlooks the total inadequacy of the social structure itself. As Foulkes and Prince (1969) have put it, social psychiatry is still a discipline in the making. The question is, where and how to start? Pious intentions are not enough. Social insight can only emerge in an operational setting. Context is a prime consideration—context that relates to meaningfulness.

The small group, by its very nature, displays only the most fragmentary evidence of social dynamics. To apply small-group or psychoanalytic models to the large group is like trying to play Ludo on a chessboard.

The large group, on the other hand, offers us a context and a possible tool for exploring the interface between the polarised and split areas of psychotherapy and sociotherapy (Caplan, 1964). This is the area of the inter-group and of the transdisciplinary, where a crossfire between distinct hierarchical structures—that is, the nursing and medical disciplines—can occur (Menzies, 1970). Where these structures have succumbed to the sclerosis of their own "sanctions from above", they become impervious to each other's "lateral sanctions". They become impervious, too, to their own and each other's informational resources.

If we are to progress, it is essential that we differentiate clearly between this new approach to the large group as distinct from the loosely structured organisations that we are already familiar with, such as therapeutic communities, ward meetings, social club, community and staff meetings, plenary meetings, communes, etc. This is new territory, which is relatively unexplored and entails the intensive and extensive exploration of large, face-to-face, "primary" groups *per se*—a meeting of the same members regularly over a considerable time, and not simply a sudden short burst of meetings, however "marathon".

It is proposed these meetings be as rigorous as any psychoanalytic or group-analytic setting, freed of current community ties and of redundant hierarchical strictures. Such a setting could provide a melting pot, an opening of otherwise impervious and closed barriers.

What is needed is a deeper understanding of the phenomena of the large group itself, in its own terms, as a developing and self-regulating system, and this mutual knowing of each other interexperientially, intersubjectively, developed to its fullest extent, might lead also to an expanding of consciousness, since consciousness itself is, by derivation, a process of knowing with others. Within this situation, one might gain experience of those ephemeral, and, to a great extent, ignored, contextual features of climate, ambience, atmosphere, ethos, drama, attitudes, and ideologies that are so characteristic of the micropolitics of the large group, and which play such an enormous role in matters of morale, communication, and information flow. These characteristics are quite distinct from similar processes taking place in small groups, in that for the first time we have a context in which outsight or social insight can develop *per se*, not only into personal social behaviour in the fullest sense, but into a questioning of current social assumptions which are so assumed as to be often totally unconscious, in the manner that a person is often totally unaware of his own accent.

The large group has two very powerful aspects and, given the opportunity, an equally powerful capacity to contain and convey its own power. In the first instance, it has an enormous capacity to generate emotion, which can very easily become ungovernable, either in the form of splitting in uncontainable panic or in the form of spilling over emotions which are irrelevant, inappropriate, and ephemeral. In the second instance, the large group is, above all, a highly sensitive thinking apparatus given the necessary time and place to evolve its matrix or organisation, communication, and containment—of which language is a typical example. Each large group can learn to develop its own containing network, can discover its own thinking potential. The "containing" is of lateral, affiliative, "on the level" communication when an expansion of consciousness, of mindfulness, emerges and grows if given the time and opportunity. The system becomes freed of redundant hierarchy in favour of self-regulation, away from mindless, crushing, Machiavellianism of manipulations through coercion and power (Watzlawick, Bavelas, & Jackson, 1967). It has its own currency and styles of control and guidance in the micropolitics of such strategies as silence, ridicule, boycott, ignoring, punctuating, timing, stimulating, promoting, in atmospheres which can, on occasion, be "cut with a knife".

It is these and other manifestations of large-group processes that we are hoping to explore more fully in their own operational setting.

Definition of the large group

For convenience, I would suggest that social systems be broken down into the following categories (Bertrand, 1972).

A. Primary (face-to-face) structures

1. Small groups from 3–20 people.
2. Large groups from twenty upwards, such that people can directly hear and see each other.

B. Secondary structures

1. Multiple group structures, complex organisations of all sorts, often only very tenuously related, for instance through "interstitial groups", such as smaller communities.
2. Larger communities—"the community".
3. Societies, nations, and, larger still, total social systems.

It is large groups (A2) that we shall be concerned with here, ranging for purposes of psychotherapy from between twenty and, let us suggest, 100 people seated in a two-tiered circle, the same members meeting at least once a week for 1½ hours (de Maré, 1972a). Until recently, large groups have been treated very much as secondary, peripheral phenomena and very much less rigorously than small groups, being viewed as supplementary adjuncts in such procedures as social clubs, ward meetings, community meetings, therapeutic committees within extremely haphazard and tenuous networks. The very self-evidence of the background scene of the large group seems to have obscured its significance. However, interest is growing in this topic, which might very well mark an important breakthrough therapeutically and operationally speaking: for instance, as a possible technique in the treatment of psychotic anxiety and in such conditions as phobic states where panic—typically a large-group phenomenon—can be handled within the individuals concerned.

History

Interest in the large primary group in a more general way has, of course, a very long history, using the word primary as primarily face-to-face. Mankind, having progressed through various phases—pagan, religious, philosophical, scientific, psychological—is now at the brink of a growing sociological awareness of social based insight that might well prove crucial for psychotherapy ("Knowing something in oneself with others") if practised operationally in a large-group setting. It would follow that the construct of the group mind would be a more consistent concept than that of the individual mind. The unconscious mind, in that case, is the mind that is not shared, presumably conscious to some individuals, but not to others.

The Ancient Greeks, with their large face-to-face meetings in the circular amphitheatres of their *poleis*, seating several thousand, any one member of which could be clearly seen and heard, laid stress with remarkable clarity on the principle of *Koinonia*. My Greek friend, Thalia Vergopoulo, tells me that *Koinonia* is a sort of spiritual-cum-human participation and communion (for instance Holy Communion), fellowship generally, and that people who are *Koinonicos* relate truly, as distinct from *Cosmicos*, who will relate superficially and more sentimentally, in a *mondaine* manner. The Greek chorus in the centre of the amphitheatre during the plays represented the *Koinonia* feeling ethically, aesthetically, rather than moralistically.

The Greek horror of alienation and exile (which impelled Socrates to choose death) was equalled only by their failure to grasp the significance of intergroup or interstate relationships, which resulted in the final destruction of the civilisation.

Cooley (1902) appreciated the large primary group as the nursery of human nature. Cody Marsh's credo (1933) was "By the crowd they have been broken; by the crowd they shall be healed". In 1916, Trotter saw neurosis as a warning signal of pain in a maladjusted society.

More recently, Laing and others have described neurosis and psychosis as a measure of social alienation in terms of social oppression and violation.

In latter years, communes, therapeutic communities, and social clubs have played a highly significant role, but we are not concerned here with therapeutic communities; on the contrary, it is the intensive and relatively more rigorous application of the large-group technique that holds our interest.

Role of the large group

Small psychotherapy groups everywhere have tended to be analytically orientated. Foulkes (1972) suggests that

> the small group, the typically psychotherapeutic group, is probably the most interesting apart from being the most valuable tool of psychotherapy, in that it is on the borderline of the two situations—it can easily be tilted towards the individual situation as well as towards the group situation. (Foulkes, 1972, p. 153)

My experience, on the other hand, has been that the small group turns more easily towards the psychoanalytic and psychodynamic intrapersonal dimension than towards a specifically group-dynamic orientation, and that group dynamics have not yet been utilised to their full extent, since it will only be in the larger group that their full potential can be shown. Although Foulkes appreciates the power that a large group might have and cites famous political demagogues, he considers that the new thinking such an enterprise requires already came into being with the creation of the small group, "each situation emphasises phenomena of a different kind, but the old phenomena are still present in the new setting" (ibid., p. 154).

This I doubt, and, since these phenomena have never yet been investigated in the new context, I think it is altogether too sweeping. In any case, Foulkes considered that the possibility of a large group meeting daily for two hours over a period of two years as more in the realms of fantasy and doubted whether this would ever be carried out in the rigorous sense I suggested. He also considered that the question of size is a relative one, and that one would require to supplement the large-group experiences in smaller groups or individually. He did add, however, that it would constitute an interesting experiment. He is aware, too, that such a large group under these conditions brought psychotic mechanisms and anxiety to the fore—which, incidentally, already suggests a striking distinction. However, in the course of further discussions, he has evinced an interest in the possible implications of the large group *per se*.

Freud was profoundly interested in the psychoses for their relevance to the understanding of the psychoneuroses. Neuroses presuppose a relatively developed ego structure capable of repression, displacement, rationalisation, reaction formation, and sublimation. In psychosis, on the other hand, the ego structure is itself undeveloped and resorts to splitting rather than repression, with projection and introjection incapable of the work, the capacity of negotiation evident in neurotic symptoms and dreams. Similarly, in any new large group at an early stage of development, contributions carry some of the character of a schizophrenic thought disorder. Unlike the schizophrenic, however, is the capacity and openness to learning secondary process equivalents, the containing of primary process equivalents by learning how to negotiate communication, how to order and organise through developmental as distinct from magical processes. The schizophrenic is like an arrested large-group process within the individual psyche, like the splinters of the mirror in Hans Andersen's tale, *The Snow Queen.* Perhaps we are, indeed, on to the fringe of a technique that could shed light on psychotic and phobic anxiety.

I must admit that, in order to make the point, I put the suggestion in caricature form, to the effect that while psychoanalysis delivered us from the limitations of organic psychiatry and group analysis has liberated us from the constraints of psychoanalysis, the large group might do likewise in relieving us of the constrictions of the small group, that the large group is a totally different proposition, and I suggested a situation for large-group therapy entailing 20–100 people seated in a one or two-tiered circle, that the structure of the meetings be arranged as rigorously and intensively as in the psychoanalytic or small group setting—certainly not less so, and recommended as an example closed daily meetings of 1½–2 hours duration over a period of two or more years.

In fact, on a much more modest scale at St George's Hospital (London), I am currently collecting a list of predominantly phobic patients who will, I hope, be meeting for 1½ hours once a week for as long as seems feasible, inviting several conductors to join me, with the proviso that the group, once started, will be closed and the participants will be expected to attend regularly.

I do see the large group as playing an antithetically distinct role from that of the small group, introducing distinctions that are quite specific to it. While the small group only too readily lends itself to a psychodynamic approach, usually psychoanalytic, the large group manifests characteristically group dynamic features. In the small group, the individual self-system is much more actively involved along a time-based, "vertical" or hierarchical dimension which concerns the personally repressed with transference phenomena from the "there and then". In the large group, on the other hand, the lateral or horizontal spatial dimension of the "here and now" is involved, manifesting "topological" phenomena such as splitting, projection, and displacement, which is transpositional rather than transferential, that is, a transposing of total worlds of contexts, environments, positions, and settings, as distinct from a transferring of the relationships within these settings. This involves total social situations without regard for present or past, involving total cultures, climates, and value systems with specific ideologies and ethos.

The amplifying and totalising effect of the large group is most striking, and emotions sweep like a breeze throughout the entire group, altering the atmosphere, rather as biologically (the energy of a system acts to organise that system) (Morowitz, 1968).

While the problem for the member of the small group is how to feel spontaneously, for the large group, it is primarily how to think. Freud pointed out the dilemma of having to procure for the group (and he referred to large groups) precisely those features that are characteristic of the individual and that are extinguished by the formation of the group. Similar experiences are described by Bion in referring to the numbing sensation that groups, at times, create in the therapist. While the problem for the individual and for the small group is the intrusion of unconscious factors (Bion (1961) has called them basic assumptions), for the large group, it is consciousness itself that is at risk, or the group's equivalent of consciousness, which is communication and organisation. The problem for the large group is its mindlessness (de Maré, 1972b).

The technique of large-group psychotherapy, which would seem to be a self-evident procedure, meets with the suspicions once accorded to psychoanalysis and, later, to small-group psychotherapy; the reasons for this would seem to relate to this very characteristic of the powerful, unpredictable, and potentially chaotic emotions stirred up in such a setting, releasing psychotic type anxiety. Once this becomes more contained and organised, it can have powerful political repercussions. The impact of the large group on its environment is indeed very much more in evidence than that of the small group or the psychoanalytic situation which takes place behind closed doors; witness the precarious careers of certain therapeutic communities (Henderson, Forest House, Halliwick "House", and the Paddington Day Hospital), threatened or even destroyed by political and administrative interference.

It is quite clear that an enormous potential of information lies vested in the large group. The tragedy is that its flow only too easily becomes blocked by all sorts of pressures, coerciveness, energy generally in the form of power and authoritarianism. Intelligence succumbs to coercion; hierarchical pyramids, far from being flattened, grow even higher, affiliative communication gives way to hierarchical blocking, leadership of ideas and trends give way to the pressure of personalities in authority and "leaders", obfuscation rules the day and the large group, rather like a large vulnerable animal, is subjected to all sorts of violations, when it is. in fact, a most highly sensitive instrument whose enormous potentials we can at present only very dimly envisage. I am reminded of the treble and bass clef in music; often the bass clef is the carrier of a mechanical rhythm; it is only comparatively recently that it has been considered as a provider of melody in its own right, not simply repetitiously, but contrapuntally in relationship to the treble clef, which, in turn, is able to follow up more readily the implications of the rhythm for the composition as a whole.

While psychoanalysis deals with matters of personal insight with relatively little political ramifications, and while group analysis has perhaps special relation to that hierarchy of all hierarchies, that is, the family, large-group therapy could have considerable micropolitical significance in providing a new type of insight into factors that remain outside the orbit of psychotherapy, notably that of social insight; in fact, most scientific discourse in psychology seems to be designed to ignore the socio-economic context in which psychological factors play their part. In certain countries, one feels the group therapists are compelled for political reasons to adopt a stringently psychoanalytic stance, maintaining, therefore, a strictly neutral "academic" position, since social insight acts as a two-way mirror—not only into the individual's social behaviour, but into the social situation around us (Brown, 1973).

There are, too, considerable conceptual implications when one considers the possibility that consciousness itself is a social phenomenon, "Knowing things with other people", so that the social context is often so completely assumed as to be completely unconscious. The split between the kindliness of individuals and the callousness of "the system" is only too frequently seen—let alone society's seemingly psychotic type of behaviour in the sense that an individual behaving in the manner society adopts would be considered insane.

Lacan (Wilden, 1972) has put it that the Freudian unconsciousness is the discourse of "the other", and Wilden has said that information divested of context is so much noise, since all knowledge has politico-economic bearings. To leave out the social context leads to a logical flatness and to the loss of the all-important factor of ethos, in which attitudes and ideologies make themselves evident not as cloudy idealistic non-sequiturs, but as crucial and clearly definable climates that either impair or promote the flow of communication and information. While in the individual setting it is the intrusion of unconscious factors that are the problem, for the large group, it is the equivalent of consciousness (communication and organisation) that is threatened; the communicational network or social matrix can either block or contain information flow and the problem is the mindlessness of inadequately evolved hierarchies where rudimentarily developed networks (affiliative, lateral, on the level) have succumbed to over-developed, inappropriately evolved hierarchies (vertically structured to prevent violent collisions and, unfortunately, communication as well).

Control and structuring are the group's equivalent to mentation and become organised as a response to frustration, hate, and aggression occasioned by the situation. The large group, through lack of opportunity, might have to resort to an overly developed control by hierarchy. This easily becomes an abuse of hierarchy, resulting in mindless and dehumanised organisations. Oppression, as distinct from negotiation, provokes hate, anxiety, and then depression in the individual. The interface at the boundaries of these hierarchical or compartmentalised areas becomes split or closed to information flow instead of negotiable and open. In this context, Levi-Strauss's nature and culture could be seen as a dialectic between hate and hierarchy. Given the time and opportunity, a group culture can develop. It is this cultural (thoughtful) potential of the large group that should be our concern and that we should aim to nurture in setting up a large group. It is this, too, which is incidentally psychotherapeutic.

The social matrix is a useful construct because it refers to the ongoing processes of a growing communicational network. Where it is only at a rudimentary stage, spilling over and splitting in violence and panic occur, but this is only evident in the early phases. "Where chaos was, there shall matrix be!" While panic fragments and stampedes intelligence, hate unites and constitutes the group's driving power for organising, communicating, and thinking, provided it does not become crushed by reactive hierarchical strictures. The hierarchy to end all hierarchies is that of the family. Unfortunately, the tendency to repeat this setting at certain stages in large groups is enormous, structures that are neither realistic nor gratifying. The members are then faced with the task of reshaping it. This is an example of the changing shapes which are so characteristic a feature of large groups and which Buckley (1967) has called morphogenesis. Invisible intrapersonal barriers are projected as more tangible constellations that the members, having imposed them, have therefore to reshape. In the large group, this differs from the small group in being so much more amplified, so much more manifest. What has to be maintained, if growth and therapy are to occur, is a permeability at the interface of the hierarchical levels; the intrapersonal hierarchies of ego, superego, and id can, thereby, undergo an active process of revision and redefinition through the group members' work of reorganising the structure of the large group itself. A better word for it would be meta-structure, or culture, since it refers to factors other than time–space and number.

A typical and often repeated phenomenon is the manner of talking in large groups. What occurs is that in the first meeting only a minority speak, as if the anxiety of talking in such a large assembly could not be contained—an anxiety that, for many people, is so acute as to border on panic. As the meetings proceed, more and more members take part and gradually the silent majority becomes a silent minority, until even they participate. This constitutes a very active exercising of the ego to handle and contain anxiety, which, since it is a situation which provokes anxiety rather than represses it, is a form of learning therapy. The repressive force is externalised into the presence of the large group as such, so that in learning to cope with this and with the often overpowering emotions stirred up by this setting, the individual ego learns gradually to talk and think spontaneously, which, in turn, creates and exercises an enormously enriched and thought-provoking situation in the large group itself. In staff groups, for instance, the members are able to jump the hierarchical barriers within and between the disciplines, and the informational gold mine that lies vested in the nursing staff can be shared (de Maré & Kreeger, 1974).

The following are verbatim comments by a severely phobic patient and are worth quoting as an illustrative example of primarily large-group feeling:

> It seems that you withdraw into your body and feel so intensely your feelings that you appear to be overwound inside and cannot cope with anything outside of yourself, the eyes and ears are outlets to a strange, frightening place overpowering your feelings, something you try to escape from, yet desperately want to belong to. I long to remember how it was to be outside of myself, living outside of my body, not wondering how my body is going to react to outside pressure, but for my body to accept living outside of myself as normal. It is like being locked up in a cell and being punished while, outside through the window, I can see people happy, normal and, better still, contented, making a success of life, and I have a key to my cell somewhere, but it's very hard to find. Sometimes I find the key and escape for a while, it seems so perfect, but then I realise that when I'm outside I do not belong there—I am still on my own, I try to get among the people and sometimes I become part of the crowd, but I cannot find anyone amongst them who seems to care whether I'm there or not, I just seem to stay an outside member of the crowd and so, against my will, I return to my self-made cell to die a little more inside, and also to start looking for the key so that I can try once more outside. I do not know if the pain of going outside is worth it, but I feel I must for three reasons. The first is that perhaps things might alter outside for the better, secondly I detest myself as I am, and thirdly, if I remain locked up inside for too long I feel I shall mentally die. If you know of anybody who needs affection and thus can help me stay outside I deeply stress, please help me to get to know them, but please don't ask me to join any clubs because I will still be on the outside looking in.

There seem, then, to be three ways of thinking. First, there is a process of finding out what the general opinion appears to be and "thinking it", a form of posturing; second, experiencing one's own impressions exclusively as half-formulated thoughts, which leads to idiosyncrasies and insularity; third, expressing these and testing them out against what other people are thinking through mutual exchange, and constituting an extension of consciousness.

The large group, in its early phases of existence and thinking, appears to be experienced as a persecutory environment that is oppressive to the individual members, who do not feel free enough to breathe ("spiritual") or inspired enough to express their half-thoughts spontaneously. This suffocating oppression leads to a depressive state, or, alternatively, to an unthinking euphoria of evasiveness, the price of involvement with, and "belonging" to, the group at that particular time. The alternative is not to belong at all—"Every man for himself!" and "Panic stations!" So, which is it to be? Security and depression? Or freedom and panic? Claustrophobia or agoraphobia?

The negotiation of a way across this gap, the working through and the infiltration by the delicate filaments of communication between the interface of these two worlds, constitutes, among many other factors, psycho-social therapy.

The large-group situation needs to be set up, and the time, the regularity, the encouragement, and a suitable locus established. Alas! too often this does not occur. Individuals in themselves repeatedly break away and never succeed in passing through these early phases, never experience anything further, but move to another setting that is then repeated, and their problems fail to be worked through. The repeated groups remain non-living, immutable constellations, unproductive, unrealistic, and closed to both the personal exchange or environmental influences.

References

Bertrand, A. L. (1972). *Social Organization*. Philadelphia, PA: F. A. Davis.

Bion, W. R. (1961). *Experiences in Groups*. London: Tavistock.

Brown, P. (1973). *Radical Psychology*. London: Tavistock.

Buckley, W. (1967). *Sociology and Modern System Theory*. Englewood Cliffs, NJ: Prentice-Hall.

Caplan, G. (1964). *Principle of Preventive Psychiatry*. London: Tavistock.

Cooley, C. (1902). *Human Nature and the Social Order*. New York: Scribners.

De Maré, P. (1972a). *Perspectives in Group Psychotherapy*. London: Allen & Unwin.

De Maré, P. (1972b). Large group psychotherapy: a suggested technique. *Group Analysis*, 5: 106–108.

De Maré, P., & Kreeger, L. C. (1974). *Introduction to Group Treatments in Psychiatry*. London: Butterworth.

Foulkes, S. H. (1972). Correspondence in *Group Analysis, November*: 153–155.

Foulkes, S. H., & Prince, G. S. (1969). *Psychiatry in a Changing Society*. London: Tavistock.

Jaspers, K. (1963). *General Psychopathology*. Manchester: Manchester University Press.

Levi-Strauss, C. (1949). *The Elementary Structures of Kinship*. London: Eyre & Spottiswoode.

Marsh, L. C. (1933). An experiment in the group treatment of patients at the Worcester State Hospital. *Mental Hygiene, 17*: 396–416.

Menzies, I. (1970). *Social Systems as a Defence against Anxiety*. London: Tavistock Pamphlet, No. 3.

Morowitz, H. J. (1968). *Energy Flow in Biology*. London: Academic Press.

Trotter, W. (1916). *Instincts of the Herd in Peace and War*. London: Ernest Benn.

Watzlawick, P., Bavelas, J. B., & Jackson, D. D. (1969). *Pragmatics of Human Communication: A Study of Interactional Patterns, Pathologies, and Paradoxes*. London: Faber.

Wilden, A. (1972). *System and Structure*. London: Tavistock.

CHAPTER SEVEN

Koinonia: a historical note*

Patrick de Maré

B y "Greece" or "Hellas", the classic world, is meant all lands occupied in antiquity by peoples speaking a dialect known as "Koine", literally "common", not the classical Greek of Herodotus and Theucydides, but the vernacular of spoken Greek, a sort of carthorse of a language, homely, belonging to everybody because it belonged to no one. It was spoken during the time of which Shelley wrote:

> The period which intervened between the birth of Pericles (495 BC) and the death of Aristotle (322 BC), undoubtedly whether considered in itself or with reference to the affect that it has produced upon the subsequent discoveries of civilised man, is the most memorable in the history of the world. (Shelley, 1939, quoted in Livingstone, 2005, p. 251)

The main structural feature of this phase in history was characterised by a novel cultural constellation, that of democracy, the temporary ascendancy of large group and citizenship over small group oligarchy and aristocracy. It failed in 414 BC, when over half the citizens

---

*This chapter was previously published in 1982, in *The International Journal of Therapeutic Communities*, 3(2): 108–109.

of Athens were either killed or enslaved in the unsuccessful attempt of Pericles to work for peace by preparing for war, finally falling prey to the oligarchic dictatorships of Sparta, Macedonia and Rome.

Athenian democracy, established for "deliberation" by Pericles, waged a battle against oligarchy. Every citizen had a right to vote at the Ekklesia or Assembly, to which, owing to all sorts of logistic reasons, only a fraction of the total population of 43,000 attended, rarely more than 2,000–3,000, mainly, therefore, those citizens who resided in Athens itself, thereby gaining ascendancy over the "conservatives" who were scattered throughout the estates of Attica. Its procedures, of course, had vital defects for which the Athenian democracy had finally to pay dearly, such as the encouragement of demagogy, rhetoric, the wasteful ostracism of able men, and the lack of organisation.

Such was Athenian democracy, "the fullest in history", "capable of releasing energies that lifted Athens to one of the peaks in history". "Never before or since has political life, within the circle of citizenship, been so intense or so creative." "The City" (wrote Simonides) "is the teacher of the man". The voter was able to listen to the cleverest men in Athens.

The circular formation of the valleys, round which the citizens sat on benches in the sun, constituted a natural amphitheatre, and, in Sparta, a rocky Epidaurus, the healer Asclepius established the most famous amphitheatre of all, built by funds from fees and gifts of patients, in which the centre, a spacious circle paved with stone (the "orchestra") faces 1,400 seats in rising tiers where everyone could, and can still, speak quietly to the farthest seats 200 feet away.

It was in this climate of democratic exchange in large groups that the word Koinonia was first coined, a term used in the Acts of the Apostles (Acts 2:42; 4:32–35; 5:12–16, The Bible, 1977). It refers to an atmosphere of impersonal fellowship rather than personal friendship, of spiritual-cum-human participation in which people could speak, hear, see, and think freely, a form of togetherness and amity with a pooling of resources that occurred, for instance, in the breaking of bread. To this day, Communion in the Greek Orthodox Church is referred to as Koinonia.

It is a sobering thought that not only the resolution of neurotic conflict, but the fate of our entire civilisation ultimately depends on our ability to achieve Koinonia.

Note

Acknowledgements to Fathers Michael Kelly and James McGlinchey

References

Livingstone, R. W. (2005). *The Legacy of Greece*. Oxford: Clarendon.

The Bible (1977). *The New Oxford Annotated Bible: With the Apocrypha, Revised Standard Edition*, H. May & B. Metzger (Eds.). New York: Oxford.

CHAPTER EIGHT

Large group perspectives*

Patrick de Maré

T he large-group approach enunciates a radical metamorphosis in our thinking about groups. It introduces a dimension that, until now, has been denied as defensive, notably the crucial role of culture as an active ingredient in psychotherapy. In effect, neither psychoanalysis nor small groups are in any position to confront universal cultural assumptions, so that, as a result, therapists become submerged by cultural influences of which they are relatively unaware. It is only in larger groups that a specific mini-cultural dimension begins to appear that can act as a standpoint from which to look at the socio-cultures and personal sub-cultures that surround us all.

Where do we start? Approaching a large group of people is like approaching a mountain. It demands as much, if not more, attention to detail as that accorded by psychoanalysis and to small group analytic psychotherapy. The emphasis, however, is different, most striking, of course, in the size of the group itself, which focuses on matters that are not and cannot be covered by small groups, in effect,

---

*First presented as "The Ninth S. H. Foulkes Annual Lecture", and published in 1985 in *Group Analysis*, 18(2): 79–92.

on cultural content. Thereby, it goes in the opposite direction from psychoanalysis and small-group therapy, since, as distinct from socialising the human individual, it attempts to humanise society.

The large-group approach, such as we have chosen here, does, however, adopt many of the principles evolved by Foulkes' small-group approach, such as the single-circle seating arrangements and the non-directive aprogrammatic setting, which is convened, rather than led, by a conductor.

But, you may ask, why a large group at all? Surely we have enough in small groups? The answer lies in the fact that psychoanalysis, in deliberately isolating the patient from a social to a psychotherapeutic frame, is a psychology of the individual. Small groups, on the other hand, invoke the psychology of the family. It is only in the larger group that cultural dimensions can be comprehensively explored.

When Freud wrote, "Where a strong impetus has been given to group formation, neurosis may diminish and in all events temporarily disappear" (Freud, 1921c, p. 95), he was treating socio-cultural matters as temporary and secondary; he thought that some day someone else would have to "venture upon research into the pathology of whole civilized communities" (Freud, 1953, pp. 141–142). His own unique and startling contribution to psychology was to remain that of the unconscious mind when the context of the outer world is deliberately excluded and reality largely rests in the person of the analyst himself.

In contrast to this there is, of course, a long history of ideas about consciousness, all of which spring from the basic concept that consciousness is mutual knowledge. The word is derived from the Latin word *conscius*, meaning (quoting from the *Oxford English Dictionary*) "knowing something with others" (*Oxford Dictionaries Pro.*, 2010). In 1912, the sociologist George Mead described consciousness as the "importation of the socialization of the outer world" (Mead, 1912, p. 57); "self-awareness of one's place in the social order" (ibid.). William James described consciousness as a unity, as a stream; and Durkheim postulated a "group mind", "collective awareness", which was taken up by William MacDougall. In the opposite direction to this, Wilfred Trotter postulated a social or herd instinct and wrote it was this that enslaved the individual by "the mere painted canvas of habit, convention and fear" (Trotter, 1919, p. 256), by "the sterilizing influence of the Herd" (ibid., p. 257). He said that the only hope was "through a slow elevation of the general standard of consciousness" (ibid., p. 259) and, in 1919, he wrote that "Western Civilization has recently lost ten millions of its best lives as a result of the exclusion of the intellect from the general direction of society" (ibid., p. 256). We see here the beginnings of an appraisal of the fact that not only the individual is unconscious, but society also, and neither one seems capable of appraising the other. Trotter further added, "Direct conscious effort is now a necessary factor in the process of a rational statecraft. The trained and conscious mind must come to be regarded as a definite factor in man's environment, capable of occupying there a larger and larger area" (ibid., p. 252).

But who does the training, and where do ideas spring from? Do they come from the gods, as suggested by the ancient Greeks, or from the unconscious mind? Or do they come, as we are suggesting, from dialogue?

Foulkes himself was well aware of the problem when he wrote in 1942 that "group therapy is an altogether desirable contribution to people's education as responsible citizens" (Foulkes & Lewis, 1944, p. 21). Professor Halsey, in the Reith Lecture of 1978, argued for "the constant need for an alert and knowledgeable citizenry to prevent the social services from serving only the private interests of public servants, *viz.*, bureaucracy" (Halsey, 1978). In 1954, Neumann epitomised the situation in his comment that "the problem lies in evolving a collective and cultural therapy adequate to cope with the mass phenomena now devastating mankind" (Neumann, 1970, p. xxiv).

If we are to progress, it is essential that we differentiate this new approach to the large group from the loose structures we are already familiar with, such as therapeutic communities, ward meetings, social clubs, community and staff meetings, plenary sessions, communes, and so on. The specific territory of the larger group is still relatively unexplored and entails an intensive study of large, face-to-face, primary groups *per se*, a meeting of the same members regularly over a considerable time, and avoiding the simplistic approach of marathon short-lived meetings, which, if anything, do harm rather than enable our understanding, and usually put people off.

I suggest that large-group meetings be as rigorously handled as a psychoanalytic or group-analytic setting, uncontaminated by communities and redundant, hierarchical strictures.

In relationship to hierarchy, I should like to quote from *The Gift: The Form and Reason for Exchange in Archaic Societies*, by Marcel Mauss (1990).

> King Arthur related how he with the help of a Cornish carpenter invented the marvel of his court, the miraculous round table at which his knights would never come to blows . . . The carpenter said to Arthur, "I will make thee a fine table, where 1,600 may sit at once, and from which none need be excluded . . . And no knight will be able to raise combat, for there the highly placed will be on the same level as the lowly." (p. 83)

When Foulkes first introduced small-group therapy to Northfield Hospital for a few selected soldiers in 1944, he also adopted a group approach to the whole hospital, but still only in the form of small groups involving activities of various kinds, including a co-ordination group. He himself acted as a link between these various groups, but there was no intergroup or large-group meeting *per se*: that is, small groups did not meet each other *in toto*, and, therefore, like a shaman, Foulkes himself represented the large group in his own person. He represented the whole of Northfield and, to that extent, Northfield did not get around to representing itself. Latterly, it is now clearly self-evident that Foulkes' principles could be applied in a larger setting, even though these would have to be distinctly modified; in fact, in many ways, large groups begin where small groups break off: for instance, rather than determining group culture, as Foulkes suggested, the convenor's function is to draw attention to the prevailing cultural assumption that the group has already created, in the manner that Bion would point out the basic assumptions the group was making. It is clear that social psychology, and, by the same token, the large group, takes the group distinct from the individual as its basic unit. It is tilted towards the socio-cultural, as distinct from the small group, which reflects the psychoanalytic and family cultures.

It follows that citizenship is only adequately observable in a larger setting, since the small groups, by their very nature, display only the most fragmentary evidence of social dynamics. To apply a psychoanalytic or small group model hook, line, and sinker to the large group is like trying to play Ludo on a chessboard. For instance, imprinting a family culture on the social context produced Freud's (1921c) "primal horde" construct, which, as he himself said, is a mythical caricature of a family writ large. Fifty years previously, Engels (1902) had already made it explicit that the "horde" is not a family institution, but marks the beginnings of social organisation.

At the second European Symposium of Group Analysis, held in 1972 at the Maudsley Hospital, Lionel Kreeger and I suggested we apply a more formal structure to the meetings of large groups, similar to the rigour already adopted in both psychoanalysis and in small groups. We arranged that the members attending the Symposium, who amounted to about a hundred, should sit in a large circle. In a burst of enthusiasm, I recommended daily meetings of fifty to a hundred people for one-and-a-half to two hours over a period of two or more years, with everyone seated in a circle and the group non-directive and aprogrammatic. After all, if it is possible for one person to do something similar in psychoanalysis, why not a hundred? I suggested that psychoanalysis had relieved us from the strictures of organic psychiatry; that small groups have done likewise with psychoanalysis, and that now the large group will do the same with small groups. I remember Foulkes treated my outburst with forbearance, but he did say he thought I was emotionally disturbed. Certainly, the tension of the meeting (and our recommendations met with a fair amount of opposition) was indeed a disturbing experience. It is important to realise that a large-group technique had not, until that time, been seriously suggested. There was no recognition that a large group is potentially intelligent and requires more structuring—more, not less. In this situation, group dynamics are in the foreground. Attitudes, ideas, ideologies, assumptive worlds, and value systems, freed of social and community considerations, make themselves evident not as cloudy idealistic non-sequiturs, but as definite cultures which can be observed as either impeding or promoting communication.

This whole question of larger groups stimulated opposition and interest and later resulted in a good deal of correspondence in *Group Analysis*. Subsequently, Lionel Kreeger edited a book entitled *The Large Group* (1975), to which twelve writers contributed.

Despite this initial interest, however, not a great deal was done to implement it. There was, if anything, a curious lack of response. Then, in 1975, I launched a large group of some forty people, which had taken three years to collect. Numbers rapidly fell to thirty, and eventually stabilised at twenty members who met for one year. In 1976, Robin Piper joined me as co-conductor and we repeated the venture, but with the important distinction that people met in a hall sufficiently large to be able to sit in a circle instead of haphazardly. This provided a greater sense of identity to the large group, which was not to be confused in any way with such meetings as therapeutic communities, social clubs, ward meetings, and so on, which, in fact, are secondary gatherings, and are totally distinct from the non-task-orientated small group of Foulkes. The name we gave to this group, therefore, was "median", rather than "large".

We found that what was needed was a deeper understanding of the phenomena of the large group itself, in its own terms, as a developing and self-regulating system, developed to its fullest extent by dialogue and leading to an expanding consciousness.

These characteristics are quite distinct from similar processes taking place in small groups, in that, for the first time, we have a context in which social insight, or outsight, as I call it, can develop *per se*, not only into personal behaviour in the fullest sense, but into a questioning of current social assumptions that are so assumed as to be unconscious, in the manner that a person is often unaware of his own accent until he hears it recorded for the first time.

The large group has two very powerful features. On the one hand, it has an enormous capacity to generate emotion, which can very easily become ungovernable, and this it does either in the form of splitting in uncontainable panic or in the form of emotions that are violent and ephemeral. On the other hand, given the time and opportunity, it can become a highly sensitive and thinking apparatus.

Anthony Wilden (1972, p. 11) said that information divested of context is so much noise, since all knowledge has politico-economic bearing. To leave out the social context leads to logical flatness and to the loss of all-important features of culture in which attitudes and ideologies make themselves evident as crucial and clearly definable climates that either impair or promote the flow of communication and information. While in the individual setting, it is the intrusion of unconscious factors that interfere with thinking processes; for the large group, it is the blocking of dialogue equivalent to consciousness and information flow that is threatened, and the problem is the mindlessness of inadequately conceived hierarchies where rudimentary networks succumb to over-developed stratifications, which are structured to prevent violent collisions and, unfortunately, communication as well, and the mindlessness of obsolete cultures.

That hierarchy of all hierarchies, the family, tends to repeat itself in large groups as a familiocentric culture that takes the form of trivialisation and infantilising. The members then become faced with the task of reshaping it more appropriately. The universal tendency to remain family fixated lends itself to creating unnecessary oligarchy and bureaucracy. As the meetings proceed, more and more members take part and gradually the silent majority becomes a silent minority, until even this minority participates. This constitutes an active exercise on the part of the ego to handle and contain anxiety, which, since it is a situation which provokes anxiety rather than represses it, is a form of learning therapy. The inner repressive force and inner objects are externalised and projected into the large group itself, so that, in learning to cope with the large group and with the overpowering emotions stirred up by this setting, the members gradually learn to talk to each other more easily. In staff groups, for instance, the members are able to jump the hierarchical and compartmentalised barriers between the disciplines, thereby providing access to an informational gold mine that lies vested in the various disciplines, for example, that of the nursing staff.

A patient attending the large group described his feeling about social situations as follows:

It is like being locked up in a cell and being punished, while outside, through the window, I can see people happy, normal and contented, making a success of life, and I have a key to myself somewhere but it is very hard to find. Sometimes I find the key and escape for a while. It seems so perfect, but then I realize that when I am outside, I do not belong there and I am still on my own. I try to get among the people and sometimes I become part of the crowd but I cannot find anyone amongst them who seems to care whether I am there or not. I just seem to stay an outside member of the crowd and so, against my will, I return to my self-made cell to die a little more inside and also to start looking for the key so that I can try once more outside. I do not know if the pain of going outside is worth it, but I feel I must try to make the attempt for three reasons: the first is, perhaps things might alter outside for the better; secondly, I detest myself as I am, and thirdly, if I remain locked up inside for too long I feel I shall die mentally. If you know of any people who need affection and thus can help me outside, I deeply stress, please help me to get to know them but don't ask me to join any clubs, because I will still be on the outside looking in.

The large group, in its early phases of existence, appears to be experienced as a bad conscience, a persecutory environment that is oppressive; the members do not feel free to breathe or inspired enough to express their thoughts spontaneously. This suffocating oppression leads to a depressive state, or, alternatively, to an unthinking euphoria of evasiveness, the price of involvement with, and belonging to, a group at that particular time. The alternative is not to belong at all and to live in a state of panic, every man for himself. So which is it to be? Security and depression? Or freedom and panic? A claustrophobic or agoraphobic response to the expanding psychic space, of consciousness?

The negotiation of a way across this gap, the working-through and the infiltration by the delicate filaments of dialogue, constitutes a form of psycho-cultural therapy.

The large-group situation has to be set up deliberately. The time, the regularity, the encouragement, and a suitable setting, have to be established. Alas, too often this does not occur and the individuals themselves repeatedly break away and do not succeed in passing through this early phase; they fail to experience anything further, but, rather, move to another setting that is then repeated elsewhere and this problem is never worked through. For the first time, we have a medium that can act as a cultural bridge between sociology and psychology and that can provide a new and third principle, that of meaning.

To summarise, then, and adopting Foulkes' method of describing small groups' specific features, I should like to list the specific features of the large group.

First, the increased size of the group constitutes a learning situation opposed to an instinctual one, involving an emphasis on meaning as distinct from gratification or reality. This increased size and soma we have to learn to cultivate as distinct from the imprintation by instinct (like a hive of bees). We have to learn to cultivate dialogue, fellowship, or *koinonia*, to affirm the presence of new members and to appreciate their potentially valuable contributions to an expanding pool of information, rather than as intrusive as a newborn, who has to be got rid of and who is of familiocentric origin.

Whichever way you look at it, the striking feature of the larger group is its size, the increase in numbers producing a definable group context in its own right: group features are in the foreground. It is altogether very much a group. In other words, it goes in the opposite direction from psychoanalysis, for, instead of excluding context, context is central. The large group is, in a way, an over-cathected illusion, as many analysts and small group therapists would have it.

It is precisely through its larger structure that there is a potential increase of psychic space, with a resulting expansion of consciousness, through a wider panorama of individual consciousness. That the large group is an illusion, as Bion would have it, is a small-group myth.

Second, for the first time the split between social and psychological is being bridged by dialogue. Among sociologists, there is controversy over what is a scientific, objectified approach to their subject.

Third, the large group goes in the direction of humanising society, distinct from socialising the individual.

Fourth, the increased size of the group is extremely frustrating and is a learning, rather than an instinctual, experience, resulting in the generation of hate. It is only through the transformation of this hate by dialogue that endopsychic energy is generated.

Fifth, the large-group mini-cultures have the effect of expanding consciousness, which acts as an ethico-cultural springboard that can distance itself from the unconscious biological and sociological cultures; these can then be demythologised.

Sixth, while psychoanalysis has a relatively unchanging context and expresses itself through free association, small groups have a tendency to introduce the family context and express themselves through, as Foulkes called it, group association; larger groups express themselves in terms of dialogue.

Seventh, the large group emphasises the principle of meaning as distinct from the pleasure and reality principles of Freud. It also creates the potential of outsight as distinct from insight.

Eighth, these changes in the mini-culture of the large group result in transpositions from previous cultural contexts and in transformations of energies that are not to be confused with sublimation.

Ninth, hate runs a completely distinct course from that of libido; it can create structures and organisations which finally contain a system of energy which can be applied, as in the distinction between nuclear energy and the bomb, between the bird's nest and the eggs, between the tree trunk and its branches. This constitutes the basis for the impersonal fellowship of *koinonia*, the cure-all for panic.

Tenth, dialogue is tangential and analogic, as distinct from the binary chains of digital logic. It takes the form of discursive, rather than non-discursive, symbolism; it is articulate, circular, lateralised as distinct from linear, and meaningful as distinct from causal. Dialogue has an enormous thought potential; it is from dialogue that ideas spring and transform the mindlessness and massification of the social oppression to higher levels of cultural sensitivity, intelligence, and humanity.

Eleventh, potentially the large group explores a wide range of human experiences, political, economic, class, and race distinction, which are treated in their own right as meaningful, in contrast to being trivialised as intellectual defence. Dialogue, and, therefore, by the same token, psycho-sociological conceptualisation, does not—repeat does not—reflect a defensive attitude towards unconscious group processes any more than consciousness is a defence against the unconscious.

Twelfth, the prime resistance is absenteeism, resulting sometimes in no group at all or, at best, a small group. I should interpolate here that Plato described dialogue as "the supreme art". People have to learn how to talk to each other.

Karl Abraham, in an article written in 1924 entitled "Oral eroticism and character", wrote,

> Perhaps the most important step the individual makes towards obtaining a normal attitude in his final social and sexual relationships consists in dealing successfully with his oral eroticism [. . .] Psychoanalysis has shown that in such cases in place of biting and devouring the object a milder form of aggression has appeared, though the mouth is still used as the organ of it.

Along similar lines Ela Freeman Sharp (1940) wrote: "The activity of speaking is substituted for the physical activity previously restricted to other openings of the body." Thirteenth, the individual, therefore, comes up against a mindless structure that is neither realistic nor gratifying, and it is this frustration that generates the mental energy of hatred and constitutes the basis for thinking, dialogue, and mind. Therefore, the main feature of the large group is its capacity for dialogue, which is a learning, not an instinctual, process, which is not anti-libidinal, but transformational.

Fourteenth, one of the strongest conflicts over larger group formations might be due to the fact that the blood relationship of siblings is the closest and most incestuous of all, and, therefore, the most repressed of all and the most frustrated by social structure.

In this connection, it is interesting to recall the variation of the Narcissus myth. Pausanius, a second-century Greek scholar, reports that Narcissus, to console himself on the death of his twin sister, his exact counterpart, sat gazing into a pool to recall her features by his own. He rejected the nymph Echo and his lover, Armenias, who pined away, and thereby drew upon himself the vengeance of the gods. Frazer (1894), in *The Golden Bough*, reports the widely held superstition that it is unlucky, even fatal, to see one's own reflection.

Fifteenth, therefore, what we have to deal with today, more urgently than ever before, is the mismanagement of energy and money. We suffer not from lack of thoughtfulness generated by individual minds, but from the shattering of such intelligence and mindfulness by outworn myths. Group culture could become group mind. We are troubled by the discrepancy between individual mind and socio-cultural mind. How, effectively, to haste a reciprocity between them? We pose the possibility that culture can more adequately be explored in a setting that is larger than the small group and note that Walter Schindler deliberately models his small groups on the family culture. Family conflicts of the past are resolved in the proxy small group of the present. The social dimension, he suggests, should be considered under a separate heading: that of political psychology. We would endorse this, and consider that the adult cultural level cannot appropriately or operationally be handled in the small group, but requires a larger setting with more people. Psychoanalysis and group analysis cover family constellations, but the larger group attempts to approach the community. We regard hate, like hunger, as a psychological absence and not a biological presence such as aggression.

The crucial function, then, of the large group is to transform the culture of psychoanalysis and the familiocentric culture of small groups into socio-cultural context that only too often remains unconscious by being ignored, and by boycotting those who question it.

The large group presents us with a broader span, a panorama ranging from the inner world at one end to being a denizen of the world at the other. It offers us a setting to understand the different transformations in which learning ethico-cultural patterns emerge from unconscious sub-cultures and social myths.

These patterns range from the Kleinian cosmology at one end through the Oedipus complex of the small-group culture to the social structure at the other in transformations that can, therefore, be looked at in relationship to each other; the relationship, for instance, between incest on the one hand and marital status on the other. There is much in marriage that is a successful transformation of incest; it is one-to-one, universal, powerful, repetitive, exclusive, and, if upset, results in primary disturbances. The large group, in manoeuvring a cultural transformation from hate to fellowship, plays a major role in affirming genital primacy. Genitality is two-faced; it not only expresses erotic instinct, but involves a relationship in a social setting. The large group serves as a setting that can be described as anthropology in the making. We do not need to go to Africa. It offers itself as a potential technique for renegotiation of earlier cultural conflicts, for instance, moving from home to school, from school to university, from university to employment, from the single to the marital state, or from other cultural splits such as expatriation. Marie Stride wrote "that the origin of narcissism lies not so much in self love as in symptomatic feelings of acute dread of the outside world" (1979, p. 249).

In the group, we have noted that individual thresholds of panic have been noticeably raised in the course of time, allowing changes in external lives that had previously been unthinkable; for instance, in the first year, two-thirds of the members attending changed their jobs.

While psychoanalysis faces inner reality and is intrinsic in that sense, denying context in favour of a total focusing on relationships, the large group looks at both: outwardly, at the surrounding socio-culture, and inwardly, at the sub-cultural implications of the inner world, both of which otherwise remain unconscious.

Koinonia is not an instinctual byproduct of sublimated Eros: on the contrary, it has to be cultivated and learned as a cultural process. It is not a sublimation, but constitutes a radical cultural transformation of hatred, a metamorphosis.

To ignore the socio-cultural context into which we are born is to overlook a crucial dimension. The mini-culture of the large group emerges as a result of dialogue, and only then is it able to view what socio-cultural and sub-cultural assumptions are being taken for granted. The intransigence of these cultures is only so because of their unconsciousness.

The main resistance against dialogue is the privatisation and disinclination to confront one's own primitive conscience, out there in the large group; a preference for letting sleeping dogs lie. Alas! The mythical monsters keep reappearing in the return of the repressed. A large group behaves like a bad dream, but, unlike a dream, it can be discussed while it is actually in progress.

Rousseau (1762), in *The Social Contract*, considered that the wills of all could only become the general will through the democratic deliberations of all citizens. Once, Foulkes remarked to me that when the Berlin Psychoanalytic Institute was demolished by the Nazis, the saying went that in good times we treat them, but in bad times they rule us. But it is imperative that we ask what are good times and bad times? Probably, the first sign of bad times is when free speech is itself declared unlawful.

At this point I should like to open up this meeting and embark upon the beginnings of a little dialogue. As someone said, "How can I know what I mean unless we talk about it?"

Figures 1, 2 and 3 below represent a schematic representation of Patrick de Maré's main themes.

Figure 1. The Three Cultures and Dialogue

The Three Cultures

Conscious		Conscious
Where do ideas come from?	Koinonic Ethico-culture (microculture of the large group). Ego syntonic superego. Humanised "logos".	
From the Gods?	Principle of meaning. Learning to talk to each other. Impersonal fellowship.	
From the unconscious?	Discursive speech (*la parole*). Discursive thinking. Analogic.	
From dialogue?	Ethico-cultural springboard, from which to view all three cultures. Increased psychic space and expansion of consciousness "the work of the function of speech" (Freud). Projective screen for all three cultures. "Language speaks us" (Lacan).	

If several persons have set the same object in the place of the superego as their ideal model or as their meaning example, they identify consequently with each other and develop tender aim-inhibited feelings towards one another. (Freud, 1921c)

Perhaps the most important step the individual makes toward affirming a normal attitude in his final social and sexual relations consists in dealing successfully with his oral eroticism. [. . .] Psycho-analysis has shown that in such cases, in place of biting and devouring the object, a milder form of aggression has appeared but the mouth is still used as the organ of it. (Karl Abraham, 1924, pp. 397–401).

(continued)

Figure 1. The Three Cultures and Dialogue *(continued)*

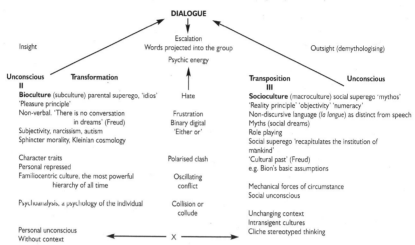

Figure 2. Structure (synchronic, static in space); System (diachronic, evolving in time)

The following scheme presents the psychoanalytic, the small-group and the large-group settings in relation to each other.

Structure (Context)	Energy	Process (Text)	Content	Meta-structure, mini-culture (Sub-text, or meaning)
I Psychoanalytic (Two person) No context Relation Dyadic	**Libidinal** Desire and gratification Pleasure principle	**Free association**	**Transference** Intrapersonal and binary, "digital", "vertical" thinking	**Psycho-biological** Egocentric Pregenital Narcissistic Subcultural
II Small group (Eight people) Oligarchic Hierarchic	**Anti-libidinal** Frustration and hate-Oedipal Reality principle	**Group association**	**Transposition** Interpersonal discursive group matrix	**Biosocial** Familiocentric Oedipal Macrocultural
III. Large group (Twenty people or more) Affiliative Polygarchic	**Socio-cultural** Mental or endopsychic energy Meaning principle	**Dialogue**	**Transformation** Transpersonal "analogic" tangential social matrix "lateral" thinking	**Socio-cultural** Sociocentric Genital organisation Post-pubertal, "Two-faced" Mini-cultural

Conclusion: Pathological cultures arise wherever confusion occurs between the three structural levels (i.e., between I, II, or III), for example, where a large group is treated as a family or a small group as a transference situation, or a large group as a two-person relationship (horde or pack), or a two-person as a large group ("Hypnosis is a group of two", Freud, 1921c).

Figure 3. Spiral course of introjected, projected, reintrojected, and reprojected objects via the larger groups matrix.

I. Introjection of the bad object into the mind	II. Projection into the larger group structure	III. Reintrojection of the mini-culture becomes reconstituted in the mind	IV. Reprojection
Frustration by external objects ("*ananke*", Freud, 1917) results in introjection of bad objects to prevent destruction of "Minding".	A. The larger group takes over the function of the superego which projectively identifies with it.	A. This-larger group mini-culture as metastructure or meaning or meaning becomes reintrojected as the ego-syntonic ego-ideal.	This recycles the next level of the spiral, recon-stituting the suprastructure of the social macro-culture towards an increasing humanisation.
External reality. The image of the hated object is split into:	B. Hate becomes bound in dialogue. The sub-culture associated with sphincter morality, oral sadism (biting), in particular pregenital impulses, become transformed into a self-regulating system of neutralised endopsychic energy, which gradually takes on a mini-cultural meaning.	(Where superego was, there shall ego be.)	The springboard of the evolving group mini-culture (specific to the larger group) enables distancing when both sub-culture and macro-culture come under observation.
A. The primitive impregnable superego, a mausoleum of frustrating objects.		B. Dialogue has reshaped the subculture (e.g. attitudes to money). Consciousness expands, and ranges from insight to outsight, achieving an affiliative *koinonic* mini-culture of impersonal fellowship.	
B. Free-floating unbound hate, a subcultural, subconscious nightmare without dialogue.			

References

Abraham, K. (1924). The influence of oral eroticism on character formation. In: E. Jones (Ed.), *Selected Papers of Karl Abraham M.D.* (pp. 393–406). London: Hogarth, 1927.

Engels, F. (1902). *Origin of Family, Private Property and the State,* E. Untermann (Trans.). Chicago: Kerr.

Foulkes, S. H., & Lewis, E. (1944). A study in the treatment of groups on psycho-analytic lines. In: S. H. Foulkes (Ed.), *Therapeutic Group Analysis* (pp. 20–37). London: Allen & Unwin, 1964.

Frazer, G. (1894). *The Golden Bough: A Study in Comparative Religion.* Macmillan: London.

Freud, S. (1921c). *Group Psychology and the Analysis of the Ego. S.E., 18.* London: Hogarth.

Freud, S. (1953). *Civilization and its Discontents,* J. Riviere (Trans.). London: Hogarth.

Halsey, A. H. (1978). Change in British Society, Lecture 6: The Social Order. *BBC–Radio 4 Reith Lectures,* 15 February, 1978 (radio programme, retrieved from http://downloads.bbc.co.uk).

Mauss, M. (1990). *The Gift: The Form and Reason for Exchange in Archaic Societies.* W. D. Halls (Trans.). London: Routledge.

Mead, G. H. (1912). The mechanism of social consciousness. In: F. Carreira da Silva (Ed.), *G. H. Mead: A Reader* (pp. 53–57). New York: Routledge, 2011.

Neumann, E. (1970). *The Origins and History of Consciousness.* Princeton: Princeton University.

Oxford Dictionaries Pro. (2010). Oxford University Press, 6 December 2011 (http://oxforddictionaries.com/definition/conscious).

Rousseau, J.-J. (1762). *The Social Contract,* M. Cranston (Trans.). London: Penguin, 1968.

Sharp, E. F. (1940). Psycho-physical problems revealed in language: a examination of metaphor. In: M. Brierley (Ed.), *Collected Papers on Psychoanalysis* (pp. 155–158). London: Hogarth, 1950.

Stride, M. (1979). Staff development in the Therapeutic Community (TC) model. *Group Analysis, 12:* 246–249.

Trotter, W. (1919). *Instincts of the Herd in War and Peace.* London: Fisher Unwin.

Wilden, A. (1972). *Systems and Structure: Essays in Communication and Exchange.* London: Tavistock.

PART III
MEDIAN GROUPS

"We will have ample cause to congratulate ourselves if we learn to substitute the law of love in society for that of the jungle and if, instead of harboring ill-will and enmity in our bosoms against those whom we regard as our enemies, we learn to love them as actual and potential friends."

(Mohandas Ghandi, 1942, p. 68)

"It is a sobering thought that not only the resolution of neurotic conflict but that of our entire civilization ultimately depends on our ability to achieve Koinonia."

(de Maré, 1982, p. 109)

"In the Median Group, we move beyond the personal and familial, entering the sociocultural domain where we explore our social myths (that is, the social unconscious). The aim is not so much to socialize individuals as to humanize society . . ."

(de Maré, 1990, p. 115)

References

De Maré, P. (1982). Koinonia: a historical note. *The International Journal of Therapeutic Communities*, 3(2): 108–109.

De Maré, P. (1990). The development of the median group. *Group Analysis*, 23: 113–127.

Ghandi, M. (1942). Non-violence in peace and war: selected texts. In: T. Merton (Ed.), *Ghandi On Non-Violence* (23–76). New York: New Directions, 1964.

Introduction to median groups

Rocco Pisani

Editing the Italian edition of Foulkes' book *Introduction to Group Analytic Psychotherapy*, I was able to get to know Patrick de Maré's contribution to the Northfield Experiment and the group analytical experiences.

The Median Group constitutes the most important development of Foulkes' ideas applied to a wider group context. To this, de Maré has given an absolutely personal and original imprint. Patrick's ideas, without suitable reflection, might even seem obscure and abstract.

In order to understand the evolution of group analysis from Foulkes' small group to the median group, it is necessary to start from the last chapter of de Maré's book, *Perspectives in Group Psychotherapy: A Theoretical Background* (1972), and to be precise, from some concepts relating to group psychology. In the last part of the above book, speaking of the third stage of the evolution of a closed small group (pregenital archaic stage, family stage, social stage), de Maré concludes that not only the outcome of a neurosis, but the destiny of our entire civilisation necessarily depends on the ability to rise to unity and achieve fellowship, or Koinonia.

Pat was inspired by primitive societies of hunter-gatherers. In a recent letter (3 May 2004), George Christie wrote to me:

In a letter to me last year Dr. Pat de Maré referred to the anthropologist Hugh Brody's recent book *The Other Side of Eden* and to a personal discussion he had with Brody in which the latter had strongly supported the contention that hunter-gatherers throughout the world, including the Australian aborigines, have met in median sized groups from time to time . . .The aboriginal hunter gatherers were open, generous and verbally honest in their interpersonal relations . . . One elder would usually be considered the leader because of his perceived superior wisdom and influence, but it would be a matter of *primus inter pares* (first among equals). If separate tribes came into conflict, a similar grouping of experienced elders from the different tribes would often meet together in a similar fashion. Such a median group council of elders would talk over matters of common interest and make decisions about controversial matters in a democratic way. Individual authentically members would say exactly what they felt; all of them would be listened to, and responded to . . .

Evolution of group analysis from Freud to de Maré

In his book *Group Psychology and the Analysis of the Ego* (1921c), Freud said that a primary group consists of a certain number of individuals who have put a single identical object in the place of the ego-ideal and have identified with each other in their ego. Everything is subordinate to this illusion: if it were allowed to collapse, it would not be long before the group disintegrated. A fundamental phenomenon of collective psychology is the individual's lack of liberty within the group. This is a leader centric narcissistic group.

Jung studied in depth the collective unconscious and the archetypes. The collective unconscious contains the phylogenetic heritage and, as the sum total of all the archetypes, it is the storehouse of all human experiences from the very first to the most obscure ones. For Jung, the process of maturation and individuation is an archetypal process that involves the integration of all the split parts within the personality. It concerns the group as a whole.

Bion's basic assumptions are a completion of Freud's observations on the masses. Bion individuated one of the basic drives for the group's aggregation in the defence of individual psychotic anxiety over splitting, fragmentation, and destruction.

Foulkes' group analysis begins precisely from this point: from the point where Freud, Jung, and Bion stopped. With the constitution of the small analytical group, composed of 7–8 members, Foulkes structures an inverse process. The conductor begins a process of gradual strategic withdrawal in a crescendo of decentralisation to the advantage of free communication between individual members (free floating discussion). So, the individuals are put in a position to acquire functional autonomy freed from the head and the other members, that is individuation.

De Maré's median group (12–30 members) is a development of the Foulkes' small group and begins where Foulkes stopped. It is much closer to the social context. Attention moves increasingly from the intrapsychic to the social, or, rather, to a greater correlation between the intrapsychic and the social. It is large enough to represent society and small enough to allow people to express themselves and to promote individuation. It is a transitional space for getting out of the kinship (the narcissistic family) and getting into the kithship (the citizenship-society).

The median group places the group culture at its centre. The emphasis is much more on the "outsight" than on the "insight" and attention is directed mainly to the clash between individual and group than to the intrapsychic conflict. The objective is not so much to socialise the human individual as to humanise the socio-cultural context. The essence of the median group is dialogue. The clash between individual and group generates frustration and hatred. The danger of persecutory attack by the group towards the individual and of the dissolution of the individual into the mass gives rise to panic of near psychotic intensity. Fear of speaking and losing identity leads to a narcissistic isolation. But if dialogue goes on, identity (the Self) arises from the Koinonic atmosphere of social interaction. Dialogue encourages the fall of the defence mechanisms and the freeing of individual expression. It allows the overcoming of the individual narcissistic barriers towards the outside world. Dialogue is levelling, non-hierarchical, multi-personal and egalitarian. Hate constitutes the basis for mental endopsychic or ego energy, which, through the system of dialogue, becomes the driving force of thought. The primary mutual hatred engendered by the larger setting is gradually transformed, through dialogue, into involvement, sharing, participation, communion, or Koinonia. Resolution of individual and group narcissism develops impersonal, interdependent friendship, citizenship. Koinonia is also companionship, coming from the Latin *cum panis*: those who eat the same bread: that is, reciprocity, mutual giving and taking, equality. Keeping tied to a dual relation of psychoanalysis (like mother–child) or to the small group means continuing to operate on a kinship, ignoring kithship with all the antisocial consequences of multiple conflicts. It means remaining trapped in the narcissistic position of the individual or the family, or the primary group (the tribe), remaining infantilised without achieving fellowship and partnership.

For de Maré "group culture is group mind". There are three cultures:

1. *Bioculture* is equivalent to the *id* of the individual mind. It consists of behavioural patterns based on the fully shared stage of psychosexual development. That is, it includes pre-Oedipal (oral, anal, phallic) and Oedipal levels, and the archetypes of the collective unconscious. Thus, we have cultures of an oral, anal, phallic or genital nature (the latter difficult to confirm).
2. *Socioculture* is equivalent to the *superego* of the individual mind (repressing, frustrating, anti-libidinal). It consists of ideologies, morality, laws, values, ideals, etc.
3. *Idioculture* is equivalent to the *ego* of the individual mind. It is the culture that cultivates the affirmation of the ego and the self.

In the median group, the clash between the bioculture (psychobiological, familiocentric group) and the socioculture (the current culture of the surrounding society) is transformed, through dialogue, into idioculture. The median group idioculture allows the bioculture drives to be expressed. It reorganises the drives of the socioculture and determines the triumph of the ego and the affirmation of the self.

As in and more than in the small group, in the median group the function of the conductor is to put the individuals in a position to acquire individuation in a more developed atmosphere of social interactions. His/her purpose is to put individuals in a position to develop free floating dialogue. Dialogue constitutes the transformative process that converts what does not make sense into understanding and meaning. It is a matter of cultural transposition rather than transference. The non-transference aspects are much vaster than in the small group. Mirroring is particularly in the foreground, together with ego–self training in action. Whereas in the small group the conductor is a transferential figure and the principal projection of parental figures, in the median group, the group as a whole constitutes the canvas on to which the superego is projected. The conductor himself supports more the role of individuals at an ego level, encouraging freedom of dialogue, interpreting the nature of social and cultural pressures, promoting and feeding the idioculture. In the median group, the individuals learn how to speak and how to deal with the emotions aroused, which becomes a very active exercise for the ego (ego training in action), which learns how to stand up to the repressive forces and emotions aroused. The individual ego gradually learns how to speak and think spontaneously. The relations between id and ego on the one hand, and between ego and superego on the other, are modified in favour of a great liberty and strength of the ego. That is idioculture.

Dialogue with the outside allows a reorganisation of the inner dialogue. The individual comes to know himself or herself through the reaction he/she causes in others and the image that is sent back to him/her (mirroring). Unconscious aspects of the self are discovered through interaction and dialogue with others. The individual differentiates through a constant comparison of similarities and differences with others. In short, the group analytical relation is expressed in a work of individuation through recognition and rejoining of the split parts of the self (self-training in action), much more than in the small groups. That is idioculture.

There are many doubts about the therapeutic effectiveness of a group of these dimensions. Personally, in the light of more than fourteen years of experience, I can give an absolutely positive evaluation. At the beginning of 1991, stimulated by Patrick de Maré's new ideas, I set up a median group in the Outpatients Department of the Department of Neurological Sciences of the "La Sapienza" University in Rome. I will present here a brief summary of the results of my experience.

In my paper at the 8th European Symposium of Group Analysis held in Oxford in 1990, I was able to affirm that the dominant theme in the culture of Southern Italy is dependence on the all-powerful and overprotective archaic mother. I concluded: dependence on the mother, deeply rooted in the culture of Southern Italy, expresses two aspects: fear of separation and of loss and fear of the devouring fusion. The anxiety of separation is perceived as panic and fragmentation, fusional anxiety as assimilation and annihilation. Fusional anxiety is concerned with the negative and aggressive aspect of the Archetype of the Great Mother, which, in this sense, is expressed in the form of witches that devour children. The positive aspect of the archetype of the Great Father, who helps the child to separate from the mother, is often secondary, or absent, or clearly dominated by the negative diabolical and destructive aspect that limits and prevents the expression of individual possibilities. The primary mother–child relationship is the common theme in the median group of patients selected from people coming from Central and Southern Italy. Fusional anxieties and those of separation are opposed to the need for emancipation and individuation. Here is a brief presentation of two sessions.

Session 24 June 1992 (sixteen attended: six women and ten men)

Content: Giuseppe's and Roberto's fusional need dominates the session; a need that is so strong that they lose their own biological male identity to acquire the female psychological identity.

In the past Giuseppe (who is homosexual) dreamed of a relationship with his mother, but she appeared as a whore who sodomised him. He describes his father as a loser. Roberto (borderline) is fully reflected in Giuseppe, though he has never had homosexual relations. He, too, had a mother who excluded the father as a negative figure. His mother let him understand that she wanted to leave his father to go and live on her own with him. The mother petted him; she kept him away from every friend. "There was just me and her and that was all." At the age of thirteen, Roberto began to dress as a woman in his mother's clothes. Giuseppe added, "When I had my first fantasy I identified with my mother and penetrated my mother. In the fantasy it was I who penetrated myself, but I was my mother." Giovanni interprets all these problems as fear of leaving the tunnel, so one remains trapped. This is his problem, too. Also, his mother had prevented him from having any kind of relationship with the outside and with others. The others agree on this theme and they confirm that the bond with the mother and the absence or insufficiency of the father is the cause of the incomplete female and male identification.

Session 27 March 1996 (twenty-one attended:
fourteen women and seven men)

Content: In this session, the Mafia appears as the archetype of the
deadly Great Mother.

The group discusses the Mafia phenomenon. As the analysis gradually becomes deeper, this phenomenon appears increasingly as a
collective representation of the Jungian archetype of the terrible
mother: the *piovra* (like a bloodthirsty goddess who must be offered
sacrificial victims and who eats children). This image emerges in
Anna's dream, in which the Mafia is represented by an apparently
male image, which, in fact, is a large woman with a big red bottom.
Also, Matteo links Mafia crimes to women, the only ones responsible
for handing down Sicilian values and culture. Therefore, essentially,
the Mafia phenomenon, though of a male kind, seems to be of female
essence, the most negative and destructive aspect of femininity. We
have the image of the giant turtle that eats its babies, of the spider's
web one must escape from, of the terrible mother whom one could
defend oneself from better by having a penis that gives the necessary
strength to fight her and destroy her. This is the infantile fantasy of
Cinzia, who is still seeking her female identity, and also of Anna and
Monica, still torn between identifying themselves as a female being or
a male identity. And it is precisely penis envy that emerges from the
fantasies of Stefania, Anna, and Cinzia as the object imagined as a tool
for defending themselves from the Great Mother's destructiveness.

The sessions are an example of how group culture is transposed on
to the group. Fusional and separation anxieties, the clash between the
sexes and the problem of male and female identity emerge as the
group cultural theme and the whole group is involved in solving it. It
is closely related to the theme of personal identity (the self). Through
dialogue, the idioculture is structured. The koinonic atmosphere
establishes the principle of meaning, or of giving meaning to communication, bridging insight with outsight (de Maré's third principle).
Narcissistic isolation gradually decreases or disappears and the affirmation of the ego and personal identity (the self) appears on various
levels according to the characteristics of the personalities, defences,
resistances, etc. of each member. From the dialogue and the meeting
of minds, new meanings emerge. So, the experience of these years has
taught me that the larger group offers therapeutic possibilities that are

in some cases superior to those of the small group. The symptoms disappeared in nearly all the patients treated. The idioculture allows the patients to reduce the negative influences of the socioculture and to express better and develop the drives of the bioculture. This finds immediate compensation on an individual level. The experience of communion and koinonic sharing is at the basis of the group and individual maturation in the genital sense, starting from pregenital cultures. Idioculture, self-identity, and mind are closely related.

In recent years Patrick de Maré, with the collaboration of Roberto Schöllberger, has examined in depth the concept of mind. In the median group, dialogue on the same level develops the capacity of each individual mind to share and develop its own reflections with those of others.

Unlike Foulkes, de Maré highlights the activity of the mind: de Maré says,

> Foulkes writes that the Mind consists of experience completely socially and culturally conditioned—and with this we cannot agree, since the Mind thinks, and is in no way completely conditioned, which denotes a passivity of mind when in fact the mind is the essence of activity in sorting out these discrepancies . . . (de Maré & Schöllberger, 2004, p. 340)

> The authentic, spontaneous thinking is a process which humanizes mind, cares and disentangles and is capable of volition, of decision making, and this is what we term the mind, constituting a significant feature in the healing process of psychotherapy. (de Maré & Schöllberger, 2006, p. 65).

That is not to deny the meaning of the Foulkes' matrix, but to affirm its importance in developing individuation, self-identity, thinking and mind in the median group. These considerations have great importance in psychotherapy.

References

De Maré, P., & Schöllberger, R. (2004). A case for mind. *Group Analysis*, *37*(3): 339–352.

De Maré, P., & Schöllberger, R. (2006). A theory of mind. *Group Analysis*, *39*(10): 65–71.

Freud, S. (1921c). *Group Psychology and the Analysis of the Ego. S.E., 18*: 67–143. London: Hogarth.

CHAPTER NINE

The development of the median group*

Patrick de Maré

T his is a history of the median-group approach in relation to Foulkesian group-analytic psychotherapy. Much of the theory reflects S. H. Foulkes' attitude, but there are also clear distinctions, notably: a new stance in our thinking about groups as a result of the increase in size (that is, to a membership of about twenty) and of the cultural dimension that this entails; and the question of what . happens after the resolution of Kleinian, Oedipal, and familial conflicts has been achieved in psychoanalysis and small groups in particular, what happens once "exile" has been achieved. It is an approach which proposes to handle the frustration and hate that these conflicts engender in the form of negative or anti-libidinal energies, and their transformation into psychic energy through dialogue leading from hate to the establishment of *koinonia*, or impersonal fellowship, and which takes into account the micro-cultural influences that promote rather than inhibit communication. Because cultural context is often treated as a defence manoeuvre against exploring relationships, individual psychoanalysis proceeds in a contextual void (the

---

*This paper was previously published in 1990, in *Group Analysis*, 23: 113–127.

analyst "standing in" for reality), while small-group analysis focuses primarily upon family constellations. The median-group approach enunciates new thinking about the crucial role of cultural context.

As to what happens once personal insight into the Kleinian, Oedipal cosmology has prevailed and the maternal and family-of-origin environment has ended, this commonly takes the form of further unending infantilisations and trivialisations; for example, dialogue in large groups is treated as a form of "play" or game. Even in the Oedipus plays, the aftermath of life outside Thebes is seen as a punitive exile suffered with the support of daughters, and finalised by ascension into heaven (*Oedipus at Colonus*).

In effect, median groups can be viewed from a standpoint opposite to that of psychoanalysis, handling the anti-libidinal forces of frustration and rage by structuring them through dialogue.

Neither psychoanalysis nor small groups are in a position to grapple with culturally assumptive structures, which, therefore, remain the preserve of the analyst or small-group therapist; they are so assumed as to be virtually unconscious. It is only in the larger context that a specific mini-cultural structure is capable of emerging as a micro-cultural springboard by virtue of its very size, sufficiently established to establish a distance (to demythologise) other cultural assumptions, such as the myths of the macro-culture of society or the subcultures from the shared unconscious endopsychic world (for example, "sphincter morality").

Recent developments

Robin Piper and the author worked together from 1975 to 1980 convening a median-sized group weekly; this has continued, convened by the author and, subsequently, by Theresa Howard and Don Montgomery, and is currently averaging about seventeen members. It tends towards the psycho and group therapeutic end of the continuum. In May 1984, under the auspices of the Institute of Group Analysis, the author started a seminar group to discuss more actively the theory and application of larger groups to members generally rather more sophisticated and more involved with theory than with therapy. This group now forms the substratum for future development of the Group Analytic Society's Large Group Section, set up by the seminar members in 1986. In May 1985, de Maré presented the S. H. Foulkes Annual Lecture. This was in effect very much a *large-group* experience; 350 people in the Methven Hall at Centre Point, Tottenham Court Road, London were seated in four concentric circles, and a good deal of interest was stimulated.

Behr (1985) says all group analysts have had a taste of large groups: "Many have even conducted them; that is to say, they have sat through them as small group leaders on a course or workshop, with no clear idea of how to intervene except to signal the ending of the session" (p. 77). Describing the present author as a group analyst who has done for the larger group what Foulkes did for the small analytic group, Behr commented that the larger group reflects our socio-cultural environment in a way that the small group cannot possibly do, pointing out that the group is not meant to provide psychotherapy for the individual so much as to contribute towards the process of humanising society. Larger-sized groups, concluded Behr, should take up the challenge and set about creating a climate in which they form an established part of our culture.

So, it appears that at long last the larger sized group approach has come to stay. The Large Group Section's aims are to bring together and create a forum for those interested in such groups; to encourage their application in a variety of institutional settings; to provide support, information, experience, and training for potential conveners; and ultimately, to help humanise our socio-cultural context through an understanding of dialogue and culture.

Median group principles

The median group follows precepts akin to those applied by Foulkes (1964) to small groups. Chief among these were:

1. Face-to-face, single-circle seating;
2. Regular meetings (usually once or twice weekly);
3. Free-floating discussion (in Foulkes' opinion group association is the group counterpart of free association);
4. A convenor who is non-directive (although capable of assuming leadership) and who remains relatively disengaged, refraining from setting topics or goals.

It is essentially an a-programmatic situation: the object is not simply *talking* ("talk for talk's sake"), but talk as an *exchange, on the level*. The groups are not communities, nor are members dependent upon each other in any external sense (contact outside the situation is minimal, and should be discussed if it occurs).

The avowed purpose of the median group is to enable people to *learn how to talk to each other*; to *learn to dialogue*. Such a principle can be applied in various situations, not simply as psychotherapy, but as an aspect of socio-therapy in schools, hospitals, industry, trade unions, housing associations, and so on. In psychoanalysis, the focus is upon the individual and the personal unconscious to the exclusion of the socio-cultural context. In small group analysis, the social context is often taken to mean the family: interpretations and understanding are formulated in family terms. In the median group, we move beyond the personal and familial, entering the socio-cultural domain where we explore our social myths (that is, the social unconscious). The aim is not so much to socialise the individual as to humanise society through a process of demythologising.

The processes which take place in the median group may, thus, be schematised as follows:

1. The individual member placed in a mutually frustrating structure of others either stays and hates, or panics and runs away.
2. If he or she stays long enough to hate (hate being, from the group's viewpoint, an achievement), he or she becomes a *membership individual*. Dialogue ensues, transforming hate into endopsychic energy, which in turn mobilises further dialogue.
3. By a process not unlike holographic mimicry, the membership individual becomes restructured, with a characteristic sense of loss of identity.

In order to preserve reality from destruction (including destruction of others), the mind defuses hate and transforms it by introjection into: (a) the impregnable superego of abandoned and lost love objects—which is a *structure*—and (b) endopsychic energy, which is a *system*. In the group, they meet together in negotiating *dialogue*. The primary mutual hatred engendered by the larger setting is gradually transformed into impersonal fellowship (*koinonia*). Running a course entirely distinct from libido, it ends up not in love but in friendship.

As William Blake wrote, "The bird a nest, the spider a web, man friendship" (*Proverbs of Hell*, ca. 1793).

The median group may be defined in brief as a micro-culture of society, with the distinction that we can address it and be answered by it. It is unique in being like a dream in dialogue, but applying unmodified principles of psychoanalysis, and small group analysis would be like trying to play Ludo on a chessboard.

Four specific features

When the weekly median-sized group was launched in 1975, it soon became evident that certain features were specific to the larger situation: these may be classified under *structure, process, content,* and *metastructure.*

1. *Structure* (or context). Compared with small groups, the meeting of the increased number of members constitutes less of an instinctual and more of a *learning* situation. Matters of meaning are involved, as distinct from gratification, and social reality matters of mind rather than of heart. Group factors are in the foreground. Instead of excluding context in favour of relationship (as in psychoanalysis), context is paramount. We explore the conscious rather than the unconscious. We have yet to learn how to achieve successful dialogue. Our median group has still to develop sufficient fellowship to affirm positively the advent of new members, and to differentiate them from a newborn infant's intrusion (that is, to learn evolvement from a familiocentric sub-culture to a social culture).

2. *Process.* Because of the learning situation (people have to *learn* dialogue like a language), frustration is a feature of the median group. The hate thereby generated constitutes the basis for mental, endopsychic, or ego energy (as distinct from instinctual energy), which, through the system of dialogue, becomes the driving force of thought. Since the communication network is rudimentary, the frustration is all the greater to begin with. In the median-group situation, the thinking process has two dimensions: the *vertical* one-to-one and the *lateral*, which takes into account the presence, minds, and experience of other people.

3. *Content.* Out of dialogue emerges a third dimension, neither of reality nor pleasure, but of *meaning*. This links personal values to their equivalent consensus in the social structure. For example, group bonding and *koinonia* could be interpreted as the transformation of the frustration of sibling incest and competition. Today, the essential problem facing us—and for which we recommend this operational solution—is that we suffer not from lack of individual thoughtfulness, but from the shattering of such intelligence and mindfulness by effete pathological cultures. *Group culture* is *group mind.* The discrepancy between individual mind and culture troubles us: how effectively to hasten their mutuality? We pose the possibility that culture can be more adequately explored in a median-group setting than in a small group, noting that Walter Schindler modelled his small groups entirely upon family interpretations (personal communication). In effect, the median group attempts to create a post-Oedipal approach. Genitality expresses not only an instinct involving a relationship, but a total social learning situation—the outcome of puberty's latency period. (Hence, perhaps, the reputed success of sexual dysfunction clinics.) Genitality is inevitably and essentially "two-faced": both biological and social.

4. *Metastructure.* This corresponds to the "superstructure" of structuralism; it is essentially cultural. It concerns the varied meanings, which the median group's context holds for the *individual,* whose cultural structure can be made manifest only through dialogue. Since the median group presents us with a broader span (a panorama ranging from the inner world to being a world denizen), it provides a setting for understanding the transformations wherein cultural patterns emerge from pregenital, preverbal sub-cultures and Oedipal micro-cultures. Such patterns range from the instinctual, pre-Oedipal, Kleinian (oral–anal) level, through the Oedipus (phallic) complex of parents and sibling, the familocentric culture (with its small-group micro-cultural systems), to the social culture at the other end.

The successive transformations can, accordingly, be examined in relationship to each other. Class distinction, racism, economic status, sexual deviation, professionalism, the assumption of attitudes and values in general—all may be explored. While the small group must learn how to express feeling, the median group learns how to express thought. Assemblages losing cultural structures either erupt into mob violence (hate) or fragment into chaos (panic); or they stultify into states of institutionalism that strangle or demand to be anaesthetised (for example, by drug addiction). Culture is, therefore, at the interface between individual and social context: it is the outcome of the dialectic between them, just as agriculture is the cultivation by the individual of the soil, or as science, art, philosophy, and religion represent mankind's cultivation of the universe. Thus, the median group can serve as a situation for exploring and discovering its own projected sub- and micro-cultures ("anthropology in the making").

The median group also provides a potential technique for renegotiating earlier contextual traumata: such as leaving home for boarding-school, going from school to university and thence to employment, changing from the single to the marital state, as well as interdisciplinary and intercultural "splits" resulting from expatriation. Fairbairn (1952) wrote that the core of neurosis is the panic of separation anxiety. We have seen the individual threshold of panic notably raised during meetings, with people making successful changes in their external lives previously believed unthinkable. In the split with reality of psychosis, the median group—by creating through dialogue a highly powerful undeniable ballast of context—establishes a reality which cannot be side-stepped, yet is, at the same time, open to negotiation.

Today's world is dominated by oligarchy. We have still to learn the praxis of assemblages; the intermediation between individual citizen and society through the "tree-trunk" of large groups—of which oligarchies are merely the twigs. We have conveyed some of our thoughts on applying group-analytical principles to a median-sized gathering of about twenty people. A similar approach to a large or global group (say of one hundred members) has yet to be explored. Our slogan might well be: "Think globally, act locally", or "Stop agonising and start organising!"

While, in small-group therapy, the conductor constitutes the main projection for parental authority figures (with the ego becoming free and strengthened by identifying with the rest of the group), in the median group, the conductor's role is rather that of *convenor*. The group as a whole constitutes the canvas on to which the superego is projected: the convenor himself supports more the role of individuals at an ego level, encouraging freedom of dialogue and interpreting the nature of social and cultural pressures. While Ezriel (1950) saw the group situation explicitly as neither more nor less than transference within a group, Foulkes was clear that significant non-transference aspects are present, notably a network of augment relationships. In the median group, we see this aspect amplified, taking on a wider range of changes with distinct qualities of micro-cultures, for example, a family Oedipal or sibling culture, a Court of Justice, a forum, or a primal horde. It is the quality of these micro-cultures that the convenor attempts to recognise, since they often constitute impediments to dialogue.

Resistances

There has been a curious resistance to this radically new development in group techniques, taking the form of so arranging matters that, in the last resort, members simply fail to attend. Such resistance is, in short, absenteeism, resulting finally in the group not meeting at all. In some published literature, resistance consists of "rubbishing" larger-group formation in one way or another; initially by limiting meetings to as few as possible—to a weekend "workshop", for example, to a larger-group "experience", or perhaps to two marathon weekends (certainly no more than six meetings in the course of a single week). One might equally well define an individual's psychoanalysis as having taken place "last Sunday".

Another variant is to allow larger-group meetings only if supplemented by a small group, akin to suggesting that small groups should only be held if concurrent with psychoanalysis. Then there is resistance represented by setting up a small group within the larger one (for example, of "monitors" or "small-group conductors"). Resistance, too, is implicit in treating the larger group as if it were a family constellation, like Sigmund Freud's primal horde, a family writ large. Apparently, Freud overlooked Friedrich Engels's suggestion that horde formation is an early animal social structure antithetically opposed to the family constellation; in other words, animals that show strong family tendencies display relatively little horde formation, and vice versa.

A further resistance is to confine the group situation as far as possible to one-to-one psychoanalytic interpretations (psychoanalysis in public, as it were). Or the situation might be treated as if it were a massive group (the Church or Army), consisting of a binary relation-ship between leader and led. Alternatively, haphazard seating arrangements might be adopted, so that there is no eye-to-eye contact, or members are left to make their own arrangements (there is, in fact, very good eye-to-eye contact in groups of up to one hundred seated in a single circle).

Yet again, resistance might lie in restricting the evolving micro-culture of the larger group itself to a limited number of basic assumptions (for example, Bion's dependency fight/flight, pairing, and work cultures). Or the group phenomenon might be dismissed as illusory: "the apparent difference between group and individual psychology is an illusion ... there is no such thing as a group" (Bion, 1961). This presumably refers to such a phenomenon as "team spirit", which, because invisible, is dismissed as illusory. Along similar lines is the suggestion that there is no emerging matrix that takes on different forms or cultures.

Dialogue might be treated as play, in order to trivialise it. Rather than take people's contributions seriously, infantilisation is resorted to, as well as over-interpretation and "scientism". Resistance can also take the form of making a sort of cattle-market—semi-organised, where "anything goes", but which in no way promotes dialogue. Here the approach is seen purely as experiential or experimental, virtually denying the rapidly evolving cultural matrix that can occur as cultures in the larger group.

A striking example of resistance to a serious approach to the larger group itself is found in the work of Anzieu (1984). The book's flyleaf states that Anzieu and colleagues "have made many advances in understanding large group situations, and these advances will con-tribute to the growing interest in this field". Anzieu bases his under-standing of larger groups upon one week's training that he provides for psychoanalysts and group therapists. During this, the trainees meet as a large group no more than six times, alternating with small groups and psychodrama groups. Some twenty-five to sixty people attend—including a team of "monitors" (present to interpret the meet-ing) and also some non-participatory observers (who, it is assumed, do not speak). With no prior arrangement either of the space to be used or its accompanying furniture, participants enter and sit where they like. Monitors move about (to "monitor") and observers likewise (to "observe"). Sometimes, large ovals, squares, or concentric circles are formed by those attending, phenomenon that appears to amaze Anzieu. He describes the monitors as "the seeds and the heart" of the group.

Several questions arise. For instance, of what value is an understanding of larger groups based upon, at most, six meetings during one week, alternated with small groups? Where would the understanding of small groups be had it been based upon such short-term experience (the same sort of time-scale as for "encounter groups" in the USA)? Why no prior arrangement of furniture: would this prevent the spontaneity of the larger group?

Exploring new territory

If we are to progress, it is essential to differentiate clearly between our approach to the median group as distinct from other loosely structured and familiar organisations, such as communities, social clubs, ward meetings, communes, and plenary meetings. This is new, relatively unexplored territory. It entails intensive and extensive exploration of median, face-to-face primary groups *per se*, the same members meeting regularly over a considerable time, not simply in sudden, short bursts, and—as in Foulkes' small groups—with no declared agenda, no goals, tasks, or directives. The median group is, above all, a highly sensitive thinking apparatus, of which language itself is a typical manifestation.

The three cultures

Referring to Jacques Lacan, Hanne Campos wrote in her paper "Dialogue and discourse" (presented in 1984 to the Sixth European Symposium of Group Analysis):

> It seems that we are born three times. First as biological organisms; then involved in and signified by a symbolic language (i.e. our mother tongue and the language of our parents and society), and finally again when we gain access to our own speech and word.

In her subsequent paper, "Group theories as the context of group psychotherapy in particular and group work in general" (Ninth

International Congress of Group Psychotherapy, 1986), she describes context as a text which permits us to give meaning a symbolic whole, so giving meaning to the words we use and therefore creating a culture. She quotes John Rickman to the effect that we are dominated by a group power of which we are not conscious, engaged in keeping within the cosy circle of the family and its simple social derivatives.

Campos summarises better than I can my scheme of three cultures (Table 1):

Table 1.   The three cultures. The emerging Self mediates and is mediated by all three cultural contexts, three aspects of a whole which can be intermeshed by the actual praxis of dialogue.

Bioculture	Socioculture	Idio-culture
	Frequently based upon the family and tribal subculture, the most powerful and primary hierarchy of all time, but also the most inappropriate.	From "idio" (to make one's own as in idiom, idiosyncrasy, "only the village idiot speaks his mind'). Personal identity. Unique, original, therefore creative; the generative order.
Sub-culture	Macro-culture	Micro-culture
Of the inner world, from the unconscious mind; for example, dreams, symbolic images, "objects", "sphincter morality". Kleinian cosmology, the Oedipus complex. The family and tribe, primary process thinking, "the imaginary"(Lacan).	Of society, usually regressed to the sub-culture of a small group psychology; familial, bureaucratic. Oligarchic, involving stereotyped cliché thinking, role-playing, non-discursive, conformist, tribal. Language as such (*la langue*); for example, "speaking six languages with nothing to say". Power structure, social machinery, anti-libidinal, anti-incestuous, generating but structuring frustration and rage by convention and hierarchy, socio-culturally.	"Existential" idios in dialogue evolving small cultural springboards from which to view other cultures, arriving eventually at the impersonal fellowship of *koinonia*, which transforms the frustration and hate into mental energy and is a source of mind, of demythologising thought, misinterpreted by the tribal and family sub-culture as exile. Dialogue is systemic as distinct from structural; it circulates, a process of self-regulation that lays down structures in the form of micro-cultures.

(continued)

Table 1.   (continued).

Material reality	Social reality	Symbolic reality
(*Mater* = mother). Non-verbal ("No conversation in dreams" Freud). Non-discursive, physiological, psychosomatic, reified, relates by identification, by fusion.	"Objective", often treated as "reality", "numerate". Like the superego, it "recapitulates the historical institutions of mankind", e.g. tribalism. There is both a social *unconscious* (e.g. myths, which are the equivalent of social dreams) and a social *consciousness* which establishes ideologies which can be either appropriate or "false".	Analogic, discursive symbolisation by words; learning to talk to each other. "Subjectivity" with expansion of consciousness ("The work of the function of speech"– Freud), Free speech, *la parole* ("In place of biting and devouring the object" – Abraham, 1924). Metaphor is not the fact ("Le non du pere, c'est le nom du pere" – Lacan). Characterised by levelling, lateralised, affiliative, non-hierarchical communication, mutuality; the symbolic order, which extends to the cosmic.
Instinctualisation	Socialisation	Humanisation
Libidinal.	Socialises the instinctual.	Humanises the social and creates psychic energy (enthusiasm). Also humanises the cosmic.
Pleasure principle	Reality principle	Principle of meaning
Mindless power. Equivalent to id.	"Humanoids"; appearance of being human, robotic, institutionalised. "Hardening of the oughteries". Equivalent to superego.	A third principle, that of individual experience. Powerless mind. Equivalent to ego.

1. *Bioculture*, which creates a subculture from the unconscious mind related to infantile sexuality, to "sphincter morality", and to the parental and family superego, governed by the pleasure–pain principle.
2. *Socioculture*, creating a macro-culture which relates hierarchy, the ego ideal, and social-reality aspects of the superego to simple social derivatives; myths which are equivalent to social dreams, governed by the reality principle and ruled by incongruous,

unrealistic, effete, intransigent, pre-conscious macro-cultures.

3. *Koinonic-ethico or idio-culture,* the micro-cultural springboard of the median group, where dialogue, symbolisation, and levelling can take place, where discourse becomes dialogue, where *koinonia* and legitimate ethical cultures emerge out of the frustration arising from the clash between sub and socio-culture. Hate is generated and dialogue transforms hate into mental energy, with modifications in the superego structure into ego-syntonic ego ideal, a culture cultivation.

Culture, wrote Lacan, is a *bouillon* of language. He said much about language, but little about groups. Concerning the socio-cultures, Campos says, "Pat de Maré has the merit of having rescued the group from the *bouillon* of socio-culture. Discursive speech (*la parole*) is essentially dialogue".

Jones (1916) constricted symbolisation only to what needs to be repressed, exclusive to the primary process, which is a narrow definition of symbol. We have, however, in agreement with Rycroft (1956), widened the definition of symbolism to "a general capacity of the mind", words themselves being a special kind of symbolism. Verbalisation is seen as a hallmark of a conscious secondary process, thinking. The three cultures represent three modes of symbolisation: (1) the non-verbal bio-cultural (Jones's unconscious symbolisation, 1916), which is not repressed but is simply characteristic of the way we think when asleep; (2) the clichés of the non-discursive socio-cultural (*la langue*); and (3) the operational, discursive talking of the idio-cultural (*la parole*).

Dialogue

Dialogue is essentially affiliative. Arguments, binary oppositions, rhetoric, polemic performances and duologue, the true and false, are nevertheless basically hierarchical or highly compartmentalised (not unlike the digital computer's binary system). So, dialogue is affiliative (derived from a word meaning "the abnegation of father"), on the level, levelling, lateralising, multi-personal, multi-polar, egalitarian, and, therefore, multi-dimensional. A hierarchical hiatus between monologue and dialogue was made by Ludwig Wittgenstein when he stated that "what can be said at all can be said clearly, and, what we cannot talk about we must pass over in silence". Wittgenstein distinguished between clear speech and silence. It is the nature of this distinction that interests us: the boundary zone in which we live and indulge in small talk and dialogue.

In the median group's early phases, there are analogies with the unconscious mind. It is a cauldron of energy in a state of chaos. Constantly frustrated, it generates a state of monstrous fury. The lack of organisation and collective will, and the contrary impulses exist side by side, without cancelling each other out. Nothing is there that corresponds to a sense of time. Any expansion in meaningful dialogue is as mind-blowing and uncomfortable as consciousness itself. As Rycroft (1979) points out, the unconscious has one positive attribute, that of being filled with energy. Otherwise, it is entirely defined in negatives. We see this energy as mental or psychic, consisting of transformed hate caused by frustration. While love *is*, hate *is not*, as it arises from frustration. Hence, the unconscious is seen in negative terms, except for this energy (itself neutral in feeling). The matter may be schematised thus:

Frustration → hate → psychic energy → thinking →
understanding → information flow → koinonia or impersonal fellowship
on the level, which constitutes a holding network or group matrix and
changes the micro-culture from persecutory to friendly, thereby enabling
sexuality to emerge as genitality.

Dialogue *builds*, arriving at conclusions in the future; it is the reverse of propositions and arguments, which commence with conclusions. Possessing the fullness and precision of the analogue as distinct from the binary digital form, it functions without final truth, having the continuous evolvement of a totalising system. It is a general way of interacting, and concerns connection, relatedness and "wholes" (both structures and systems), not being dependent solely upon the dialectic process of thesis and antithesis. It is tangential, with nuances of relation and meaning, including pauses and silences. Concerned with continuum and not simply with boundaries, it allows for different communications occurring simultaneously. It both influences and is influenced by atmosphere and cultural context. It can become open, free-floating, untamed, evocative and provocative; empathetic and rich in ambiguities; full of verbal meanings, with poetry, timing, style, quality, complexity. Being multi-personal, it does not follow the course of syllogistic logic. Dialogue uses language and transforms it. Median group dialogue, given the opportunity, can do the same to culture.

Future developments

The members of the Large Group Section are engaged not only with their own experiences within the seminars as a median-sized group (that is, learning to mediate the three cultures—*bio*, *socio*, and *idio*), but in exploring, launching, and supervising median-sized groups in several fields, for example, in a single-parents' group, a residents' association in an estate of flats, a religious order, a black-and-white group, an unemployed group, hospital staff groups, psychotherapy groups, teachers' groups, and political groups (including one on policies concerning nuclear war and national security issues).

Acknowledgement

The author thanks the publishers of *Group*, the Journal of the Eastern Group Psychotherapy Society, Philadelphia, for permission to publish this article, which is a shortened edition of "The history of large group phenomena in relation to group analytic psychotherapy: the story of the median group", published in *Group*, 1990, *13*(3–4). He also wishes to thank the past and present members of the Large Group Section of the Group-Analytic Society (London) for their enthusiasm and inspiration.

References

Abraham, K. (1924). The *Influence of Oral Eroticism on Character Formation.* Reprinted London: Karnac, 1979.

Anzieu, D. (1984). *The Group and the Unconscious.* London: Routledge & Kegan Paul.

Behr, H. (1985). Editorial. *Group Analysis*, 28 (2): 77.

Bion, W. R. (1961). *Experiences in Groups*. London: Tavistock.

Campos, H. (1984). Dialogue and discourse. Paper presented at the 6th European Symposium of Group Analysis, Zagreb.

Campos, H. (1986). Group theories as the context of group psychotherapy. Paper presented at the 9th International Congress of Group Psychotherapy, Zagreb.

Ezriel, H. (1950). A psychoanalytic approach to group treatment. *Journal of Medical Psychology, 23*(1 & 2): 59–74.

Fairbairn, W. R. D. (1952). *Psychoanalytic Studies of the Personality*. London: Tavistock.

Foulkes, S. H. (1964). *Therapeutic Group Analysis*. London: Allen & Unwin [reprinted London: Karnac, 1984].

Jones, E. (1916). The theory of symbolism. In: E. Jones (Ed.), *Papers on Psycho-Analysis*. London: Bailliere, Tindall & Cox, 1948.

Rycroft, C. (1956). Symbolism and its relation to the primary and secondary processes. *The International Journal of Psychoanalysis, 37*: 137–146.

Rycroft, C. (1979). *The Innocence of Dreams*. London: Constable.

CHAPTER TEN

The median group and the psyche*

Patrick De Maré

"Custom in a child comes to have the force of nature."

(Thomas Aquinas, c. 1260)

In *A Critical Dictionary of Psychoanalysis*, Charles Rycroft (1968) writes that psyche and mind are used synonymously. It is a little strange that the word "psyche" has been adopted, since, in fact, she was a beautiful nymph married to Eros, the god of love, and granted immortality by Jupiter. (The soul was, therefore, erotic as distinct from sexual.) She is represented as having butterfly wings to indicate the lightness of the soul. "Psyche" is also a Greek word for "breath", which escapes as a butterfly from the mouth at the moment of death.

Plato supposed psyche to be an entity separate from crass corporeal sense, and this separation is similar to Descartes's notion of body–mind duality. In relating psyche and the social world we need to distinguish between group and group spirit, in the manner of team

*Previously published in 1994, in: D. Brown & L. Zinkin (Eds.), *The Psyche and the Social World: Developments in Group Analytic Theory* (pp. 202–210). London: Jessica Kingsley.

123

and team spirit. Spirit emerges as a separate entity when an individual separates from that particular team. As long as the individual psyche is part of the team matrix, it remains attached as an epiphenomenonal side effect to that team; thereafter, it becomes mind, as distinct from brain, and can be reapplied in the form of memory in subsequent teams, or, alternatively, it can be applied to the spaceless and timeless world of non-people. During this latter state it derives energy from that cosmos and can become self-generative, while in the former it is bound to people, which is draining and frustrating and generates hate. This, in football, results in kicking the ball around, while in groups it creates dialogue. Free speech is the first to go in totalitarian states.

Psychiatry deals with the brain in a way which is materialistic (Latin—mother) and treats the brain as consisting of ever-increasingly complex reflexes. Psyche-therapy, on the other hand, treats the mind separated from reflexes, as being capable of reflection. It is a sort of brain by proxy, which develops from the moment of birth when separation takes place, the world of non-mother or of breath. Like the ancient Greeks, the Buddhists consider mind to be synonymous with breath (psyche—soul or breath).

The freedom of the psyche is squeezed between insight and outsight. It either materialises into the body or emanates into the mind; material strictures *vs.* psychic expansion; for example, Stephen Hawking, confined to a wheelchair, rises to a boundless universe in his *A Brief History of Time*. Spirit can overcome dispiritedness.

In addressing the issue of psyche and the social world, the median group of between twelve and thirty people offers us an operational approach. The small group, by the nature of its size, lends itself more to the bureaucratic hierarchy of the family culture and displays only the rudiments of social order. Foulkes pointed out that social psychiatry is still in the making (Foulkes & Prince, 1969), and it has been suggested that applying small-group principles to the larger setting is like playing Ludo on a chessboard.

Groups can be divided into small groups—for example, family; median groups, such as extended family; and large groups and global groups, society. Group psychotherapy, by the same token, offers three proxy settings: that is, small groups of five to twelve, medium-sized groups of twelve to forty, and larger groups of forty to several hundred. Each one of these settings carries with it a corresponding "mind" or culture; for example, biocultural, psycho-cultural, socio-cultural, and politico-cultural. The medium group, or median group as we have called it, provides an opportunity for each member to have his say within a reasonable time; it is a good setting for learning to talk and think, and for direct access between psyche and society.

Levi-Strauss pointed out that both language and culture "have taken thousands of years to develop and both processes have been taking place side by side within the same minds" (1949, p. 71). In the median group, we are practising and intensifying these processes operationally. Essentially, culture implies the expression of human group thinking.

It is interesting to note that while the median group, as an applied approach, is curiously lacking in modern-day society, it is universal in so-called primitive and long-standing cultures, which date back, in some instances, to over 60,000 years ago, coping with the most arduous of physical conditions. We today, on the other hand, starve in the midst of plenty because we mindlessly adhere to an economic sub-culture that belongs to the age of scarcity, before the invention of the wheel.

Small group approach

What do small-group writers have to say about this? Foulkes, on the whole, simply emphasises the authority of the small group. Ernest Hutten, in his chapter in *The Evolution of Group Analysis* (1983), wrote that the "small group provides the proper setting for our wellbeing and preserves it". He adds, "The natural organisation of human beings is then the small group, the extended family or the small herd or tribe" (p. 151). He sees the extended family or tribe as the natural and spontaneous extension of the small group, which we cannot endorse, since this is cultural or contrived development, socially determined.

In contrast to Hutten, H. J. Home, in his chapter 'The effect of numbers on the basic transference pattern in group analysis', wrote:

> The classical situation of Foulkes' group analysis requires us to see the patient once-weekly with seven others . . . two, three or even four do not quite make a group. To my feeling a group exists with five of a kind, e.g., five patients. Six, seven or eight consolidate the group and beyond that number the character of the phenomena begins to change

very slowly. At about fifteen a new character emerged, a medium-sized group, and at about twenty-five a large group. (Home, 1983, pp, 144–145)

This I would agree with, and the extended family, or tribe, must be clearly distinguished from the family group. The tribal group is cultural, not natural. Imbued with a sense of community as distinct from biological interdependence, the larger network does not function instinctively, but has to be cultivated. Thus, while the small group of strangers acts as a proxy group for family instincts, the medium-sized group acts as a proxy tribal group negotiating culture. It straddles the interspace between kith and kin, neighbour and relative, society and consanguinity.

Anthropological background

My experience has been that the medium-sized group, the median group (or the "dialogue group", as Professor David Bohm has named it), empirically speaking, ranges between twelve and thirty, Anthropologists have described such groupings as bands or camps of hunter-gatherers, ranging between twelve and fifty. The social psychologist Charles Cooley described similar groups in *Human Nature and the Social Order* (1902), which represented the first modern coverage of such groups and which he called primary groups.

By primary groups, I mean those characterised by intimate face-to-face association and co-operation—the neighhourhood and the community of elders. They are practically universal, belonging to all stages of development, and are, accordingly, the chief basis of what is universal in human nature and human ideals. Such association is clearly the nursery of human nature in the world around us, and there is no apparent reason to suppose that the cast has anywhere or at any time been essentially different.

The problem as Cooley saw it was how to build and promote primary group life; the theory of the eighteenth and nineteenth centuries of horde or rabble of basically selfish and unorganised individuals driven by animal instinct is a highly fictitious phantasy, even though it was shared by the psychiatrists of the time—Freud, for instance. In other words, there is a basic dichotomy between man and society, and man is basically antisocial. In contrast to this, the median group is a situation where the psyche can most freely and fully be exercised and is least trammelled by rules imposed on it either by the family setting of the small group or the extensive massifying effect of society at large. We see the psyche, therefore, in terms of the Greek word "idio", which means making things one's own: as in idiomatic or idiosyncratic, or idiot even. This usage represents the personal human mind gaining expression in the micro-culture of the median group. In the median group, we witness anthropology in the making.

Anthony Giddens, in his book *Sociology*, writes, "Warfare in the modern sense is completely unknown amongst hunter-gatherers".

> Hunters and gatherers are not merely primitive people whose ways of life no longer hold any interest for us . . . the absence of war, the lack of major inequalities of wealth and power and the emphasis on co-operation rather than competition, are all instructive reminders that the world created by modern industrial civilisation is not necessarily to be equated with "progress". (1989, p. 46)

He adds,

> For all but a tiny part of our existence on this planet human beings have lived in small groups and tribes often numbering no more than thirty or forty people, The earliest type of human society consisted of hunters and gatherers, . . .hunting and gathering cultures continue to exist today in some parts of the world, such as the jungles of Brazil or New Guinea but most have been destroyed or absorbed by the global spread of Western culture and those that remain are unlikely to stay intact for much longer. (Ibid., p. 43)

He is alive to the hiatus between psyche and society, where "mind", a word derived from the Norse "mynde", or vote, comes in to its own, in which speaking one's mind is equivalent to the democratic principle of casting one's vote, that is, at an age when one is old enough to be regarded as "myndig" (Norwegian).

Numbers ranging from ten to thirty have been described by many anthropologists as providing a viable unit for survival of Pygmies, Aborigines, Eskimos, and Dogrib Indians. This basic social unit of the hunter-gatherers succeeded in coping with the extremely tenuous social connections as well as with the impoverished environment. They talked regularly to no specific purpose, apparently without making decisions; there was no leader, everybody participated, and the meeting went on until they came to a spontaneous halt.

If we turn to present-day industrial society, we can ask how it can be that intelligent individuals perpetuate cultures that are destructive. I believe that the answer to this lies in the clash between the individual mind and the group mind, and, as I have already suggested, group mind is what the term "culture" implies. Without dialogue, minds are cut off from one another and produce groups that are pathological. The multi-personal transitional space (of the median group) is distinct from the dialectical triad of thesis, antithesis, and synthesis. Rather, it is tangential or "multi-lectic". In this setting, the reflexes of brain encounter one another in a constant process of reflection. Whereas psychoanalysis explores the individual unconscious, small group examines the family. I suggest the median group can address operationally the socio-cultural context in which we reside, usually as helpless onlookers. This is the essence of the problem we are attempting to resolve in practising regular meetings of the median group between individual psyches, applying the principles of Foulkes wherever applicable. This approach represents a significant development in the history of small-group analysis; that is, we are applying the same principles, but to a larger setting, This supersedes what the small group replicates, and provides a psychosocial reconciliation not only with socialisation of the individual, but with the humanising of society.

Operational approach

In Aristotelian logic, there is a polarity of "either or", between which lies an area which Aristotle referred to as the "excluded middle"; within this interface, in transposing this concept to the median group, dialogue can occur, creating fleeting micro-cultures, metamorphosing passing micro-cultural changes. This is similar to Kuhn's paradigm shifts, the crucible between family and social, where there is no root or basic culture, but a constantly evolving flow of micro-cultures of the median group in flux.

Moreno wrote, in *Who Shall Survive?* (1953), that when the Messiah comes it will be in the form of a group. For us working with median groups, this is a feasible suggestion. If twenty members of a median group after two years could each take on a similar project, within ten years several million people would be involved, and we suggest this as a deliberate strategy. This is, of course, distinct from the occasional meetings of one-off "large groups"; the theme of the relationship between psyche and society is essentially one that must be developed operationally. I am not, therefore, speaking academically, but am cultivating the hinterland between the family homestead of the small group and the massive chaos of the large group. The setting is both post-familial and pre-political. There is no root or basic culture, and we are attempting to promote "outsight" as distinct from "insight". Outsight relates to insight in the way that outside and inside relate. "Outsight" is a simple complementary term: whereas insight refers to inwardly orientated expansion of awareness, outsight refers to the outward expansion of social consciousness and thoughtfulness.

This is all done through learning to talk to one another and facilitating reciprocal transformations between psyche and society. It is appalling that, of the hunting and gathering cultures that continue today in the jungles of Brazil or New Guinea, most have been destroyed, and I and my co-workers intend to resuscitate and reclaim this approach, which is occurring not in the unyielding eco-system of the desert, but in the flourishing productivity of our present world, in which humanity has, as never before, been endowed with potential wealth but in which we survive in a manner that can only be described as incompetent.

As I have said, small groups, being family-sized, accordingly lend themselves to the family culture. By their very nature, they represent a biological infrastructure in conflict with the superstructure of society, and pose the most imbedded hierarchy of all time. They are in a constant state of mutual frustration. The median group acts as a stepping-stone, a transitional space. It is essentially a two-faced phenomenon, which I have termed "transpositional", as distinct from "transferential".

Dialogue

Dialogue, "the supreme art" (Plato), turns out to be a highly complex negotiation in the face of emotional forces that threaten to curtail or disrupt the meetings. It stimulates thinking as well as emoting.

Whereas Bion, in his work with groups, regarded hate as an endogenous and constitutional manifestation of the death instinct, I see it as a response to frustration that generates an energy that is essential in activating the mind. Like Socrates, I believe in the role of sustained dialogue, and follow his principles of following up the argument wherever it leads. This goes far beyond the hierarchy of the family. Dialogue provides a transitional space equipped to deal with psychological traumata as well as psychoneuroses, and acts as a transitional object for splinters embedded in the psyche from the shattered mirroring of previous social catastrophes. War, holocausts, and racism can be explored in a koinonic atmosphere facilitating recovery.

An example is that of a woman who had been in a concentration camp between the ages of three and seven, together with her parents. When she eventually came to Britain, she underwent small-group psychotherapy, then a daily analysis for several years arranged at the Hampstead Clinic, and then had individual fortnightly supportive psychotherapy. When the latter terminated, she developed severe depression and was referred to a median group. After a few meetings, she had a nightmare in which the members were being swamped by a wave of black, radioactive mud, and, for the first time, thereafter she was able to talk about her experiences. This is an instance of post-trauma neurosis, and only the median group was able to act as a suitable secure container, being both sufficiently powerful to contain her feelings and yet small enough to allow her to speak freely.

Conclusion

Depression, like oppression, blocks the mind; likewise, exercising the mind unblocks depression. I have come to realise that the median group is an appropriate setting for movements of this kind. Having stepped back from large and small-scale groups towards groups of intermediate proportions, I have recognised the significance of group number in influencing profoundly the character of our relationships in handling hate and fear.

The Aboriginal name for "white man" is "no ancient law and no culture", reminding us of Aristotle's comment that "he who is unable to live in society or has no need because he is sufficient for himself, must be either a beast or a God".

The median group, or "band", emerges as a self-evident extension of the Foulkesian small group, facilitating psyche in handling the social world. Like the small group, it does not emerge automatically; it requires thought, organisation, ongoing training, and cultivation on the part of the convenors. By the same token, it remoulds Psyche herself in evolving communicable micro-cultures. In so doing, there is a continuous interplay between the systemic flow of dialogue and the changing cultural structure of the group itself, like the river and river-bed.

"Koinonia" originally implied love for the state as distinct from love of family. The more intimate, one-to-one personal relationship of friendship runs a distinctly different course, and, in psychoanalysis, has been referred to as the therapeutic alliance. Friendship is a universal criterion, a yardstick against which such manifestations as transference, manipulation, and seduction can he contrasted, highlighted, and interpreted. The client does not buy friendship, but pays for the therapist's time and skill.

Psychoanalysis added a new dimension to psychiatry, and small groups extended psychoanalysis. The median or dialogue groups widened small groups and, in turn, will be further contextualised by larger groups and eventually global groupings. These larger groups arc mainly non-verbal, and cultural contextualisation replaces dialogue. As an example, a schizophrenic attempts to verbalise context in the form of a strangely depersonalised quality of hallucinatory voices.

If we are to address the knotty problem of the psyche and the social world, it is imperative that we devise an adequate and appropriate operational technique. For example, pop concerts generate a context which can replace and release young people from their past contexts. How to harness this power comprehensively and to effective purpose could constitute a major breakthrough in establishing cultural change. The problem lies in how to focus the koinonic with the friendly, since they are by no means synonymous; indeed, they are usually discrepant and, therefore, mutually destructive.

Acknowledgements

Discussions with Piers Lyndon played a formative part in my writing this essay, in honoured memory of the late David Bohm.

References

Aquinas, T. (1260). A reputation of the above mentioned opinion and a solution of the arguments. In: A. C. Pegis (Trans.), *Summa Contra Gentiles*. New York: Image Books, 1955.

Cooley, C. (1902). *Human Nature and the Social Order*. New York: Scribners.

Foulkes, S. H., & Prince, G. S. (Eds.) (1969). *Psychiatry in a Changing Society*. London: Tavistock.

Giddens, A. (1989). *Sociology*. Oxford: Blackwell.

Home, H. J. (1983). The effect of numbers on the basic transference pattern in group analysis. In: M. Pines (Ed.), *The Evolution of Group Analysis* (pp. 144–150). London: Jessica Kingsley, 2000.

Hutten, E. (1983). Meaning and information in the process. In: M. Pines (Ed.), *The Evolution of Group Analysis* (pp. 151–166). London: Jessica Kingsley, 2000.

Levi-Strauss, C. (1949). *The Elemental Structures of Kinship*. London: Eyre & Spottiswade.

Moreno, J. (1953). *Who Shall Survive*. New York: Beacon House.

Rycroft, C. (1968). *A Critical Dictionary of Psychoanalysis*. London: Nelson.

CHAPTER ELEVEN

The median group*

Patrick de Maré

The median group is a term coined by Patrick de Maré in the 1990s (de Maré, Piper, & Thompson, 1991) to differentiate between the small group and the large group. While the small group is structurally the size of the family and lends itself, therefore, to having a hierarchical and tribal micro-culture, the large group tends to be level and social; the median group of about twenty members is large enough to be social rather than tribal, and yet is small enough for each individual to be able to have his say within a reasonable time, that is, 1½ hours. In fact, it is a very ancient technique and was practised by the hunter-gatherers round the campfire; it is, to this day, still applied by bushman, Aborigines, Eskimos, and so on. De Maré is recognising it as extension to the psycho- and group-analytic approaches and as a stepping-stone to the little understood large political group, which is too large for all members to express themselves directly and individually.

The median group uses as its currency the levelling of a free-floating dialogue as distinct from the process of free association in

_____

*This is a previously unpublished paper, written in 2000.

psychoanalysis and group association in small groups, which are hierarchical, the family being the most hierarchical of all structures.

The median group represents a significant development towards introducing an operational method of exploring our cultural dimensions—it is large enough to offer a micro-cultural springboard whereby the surrounding macro-cultures can be explored and assessed. Probably, the large group will eventually be conducted not by a single convenor, but by a membership of seventeen members already versed in the median group. The median group constitutes an about-turn in direction from the small group, in that it has evolved outsight into cultural contexts, as distinct from the insights of small group and psychoanalysis.

The essence of the median group is to help people learn how to talk to each other consistently and comprehensively, and Plato called dialogue the Supreme Art.

In the course of median group experiences, it has become possible to introduce certain new concepts not previously available: for instance, no word exists bearing the same relation to the vagina as phallus does to the penis. The median group in which the binary male and female micro-cultures are explored refers to the female micro-culture as Kunta, an old Norse word.

Similarly, transposition replaces transference, involving cultural situations and contexts as distinct from referring to people.

Third, transformation through dialogue of rage, hate, and outrage into mental energy, as distinct from simply "abreaction", the evolving of mind is an agent that addresses frustration.

Finally, the realisation of the distinction between sexual (procreation) and erotic (creation). Sexual promiscuity (bodily) has necessarily to be controlled, while the erotic (mental) needs to be cultivated. (In the Greek myth, Eros wedded Psyche.)

As a technique, the median group is steadily gaining recognition as a revolutionary procedure in the uncovering of the many prejudicial and inappropriate micro-cultures that surround us, for example, starvation in the midst of plenty. We live in physical wealth, which we cannot enjoy because of artificial financial constraints, money being abused as a tangible commodity (in the form of credit) as distinct from an abstract means of distribution.

Dialogue creates the symbolic world of culture and, therefore, of abstraction. In other words, culture is group mind.

The application of the median group in high security prisons, in the Navy, and other institutions is proving more productive than that of the small group, since it addresses socio-cultural issues as opposed to stirring up the familo-tribal past.

Reference

De Maré, P., Piper, R., & Thompson, S. (1991). *Koinonia*. London: Karnac.

CHAPTER TWELVE

The millennium and the median group*

Patrick de Maré

T he advent of the millennium has stirred people up everywhere, as if something really significant is about to happen. Clearly, that Christianity has survived for a second thousand years is no mean achievement, but that does not explain why group analysts who are not specifically Christian have decided to publish a special issue of their journal about the future of group analysis during the millennium.

Nevertheless, Heulwen Bawaroska, Helen Schick, Carole Clifford, David Parsons, and myself, who constitute the backbone of what we have called the Median Group Seminar, which meets informally at my home, are absolutely delighted, since, on the whole, we feel we have been boycotted by most group analysts, intent on promulgating small groups even though they themselves constitute a large group of several hundred people.

There is another matter I should like to mention, which is that in entering the second millennium we have also encountered the potential of becoming dualistic, one thousand having become two; we have

---

*This paper was previously published in 2002, in *Group Analysis*, 35(2): 195–208.

had to reflect on our previously linear development and to think more about human affairs in dyadic terms, rather like a midlife crisis of having to discover one's story.

At eighty-five, after sixty years' experience in psychotherapy and group therapy, I have discovered a certain practical *modus vivendi*, which I have considered to be my philosophy about psychotherapy and the mind, and which I have divided under five headings, to disentangle what would otherwise be a chaotic situation: these are: structure, process, content, metastructure, and totality.

Structure

Structure refers to the spatio–temporal matters of when, where, who, selection, size, number, proximity, frequency, and duration, matters of the natural world often called physical reality. In the social sciences, for instance, Durkheim (1901) defined sociology as *the science* of institutions. It is structure also, predominantly (rather than process and content), that concerns the anthropologist. As an example from the organic, material world, structure relates to a focus on *the science* of the brain rather than the semantic meaning of the word (i.e., *control*). Structure is often exclusively monistic, "neutral monism", as Bertrand Russell (Eisler, 1993) has termed it. Structure concerns drives, logic (as distinct from logos), and figures and letters (rather than words), other associations including somatic, cause–effect, linear extension, measurability, predictability, tangibility, concrete, biological, statistical, cost-effectiveness.

Attachment theory is an interesting case in point, for, although it refers to the self-evident psychological relation of the actual mother's person in relation to the very personal and specific infant, it was felt necessary to be supported by *biological* evidence. Even though attachment theory was conceived of as distinct from sex and feeding, relating to the psychological meaning of attachment, and is what I would describe as psychic, psychological, not biological, it was apparently felt it required biological sanction.

Feeding and sex are physiological functions, while Eros is of the mind. Sex, being procreative, cannot afford to be promiscuous. Creativity, on the contrary, *has* to be cultivated, as a source of culture, inspiration, and to counteract the suffering of depression. Sexual perversion is a pseudo-solution. Freud considered perversion to be at the core of all neurosis (it can, indeed, act as an antidepressant), and that all psychopathology has an infantile sexual component. The puritan ethic throws out the baby with the bathwater, frowning on speculation and creativity. Of course, while depression is a respectable disease, sexual perversion is not, within the Puritan ethic and culture.

The linear course of the "natural" sciences, statistics, measurability, predictability, quantum theory, cause–effect, cognitive science, behaviourism, rockets to Mars, phallocentricity, pollution, are all culturally "respectable", as are the poignantly named theories of the black hole and the big bang (while the primal scene is not, except in psychoanalytic circles).

By the same token, new developments such as the median group are treated with considerable circumspection.

Process

The mind cannot be a linear extension of the brain, since it occurs between brains and is, therefore, a binary phenomenon. The mind is a dynamic process, and, in that sense, abstract, representing a counterpoint to structure. It reflects, not in the sense of simply mirroring some more solid foundation in structure, but in the sense of thinking. It concerns *the experience* of existing (derived from the word meaning ecstasy).

Shakespeare wrote that "my brain is female to my mind giving rise to ever breeding thoughts". The brain is bodily and sexual, as distinct from the mind, which is reflective and erotic (Eros married Psyche).

In the words "*Cogito ergo sum*", Descartes declared that, in the midst of a world about which little could be known for certain, *he knew* he existed, thus suggesting the primacy of mind, experience, over body, matter, and creating the duality that has caused so much controversy.

In the *Upanishads*, it is written that when the individual realises unity, he becomes liberated from the sorrow that is the product of dualities. This is forward-looking in the sense that such unity can only come through a third "principle" of dialogue and the resolution of ambivalence. When backward-looking, such "liberation in unity" is spurious, some sort of linear thinking of which mind is an extension without any change of gear—or perhaps the mind becomes in these circumstances a by-product or epiphenomenon, leading to fragmentation and ruminations of ever smaller circles.

Duality has first to become established, if we are to proceed to praxis. However academically unacceptable, the practice of therapy entails the elegance of a triadic operation. Is this what Wittengenstein meant when he concluded in his later lectures that philosophy is ever a battle against the bewitchment of our intelligence by means of language, that philosophy is only significant when it is therapeutic (in contradistinction to playing games with words); that therapy is the yardstick of philosophy?

In an important respect, duality is not yet established for us. I noted elsewhere, in a piece co-authored with Professor Stavroula Yannitsi (1998) under the title of "Phallus and kunta", that there is no equivalent word for women corresponding to the phallus of men. The word phallus is a symbol representing the cultural implications surrounding the penis, and the ancient Greeks clearly differentiated between peos, or penis, and phallus, its cultural equivalent. Freud, on the other hand, treated them as synonymous, and he went on to argue that libido itself is masculine. Lacan stated that "there is no symbolization of women's sexuality" and "there is no female equivalent to the prevailing symbol of phallus in the symbolic order" (Lacan, quoted in Miller, 1993, p. 76). This indicates that the very language we use in the West must be in itself phallocratic. The repercussions of these widely accepted assumptions are enormous. They both disempower women and, by using linear and monopolistic (mono-polar), not to say *monotheistic* and *monolithic* thinking, constrict our minds by denying dualism, the stepping-stone to dialogue.

It is imperative we discover the appropriate female symbol. Man is described as a symbol maker, and symbols shape our thought processes and cultures. The discoveries of new symbols, the changes in meaning of others, the dropping out of words from currency altogether, the alteration of myths, are common phenomena. For instance, the historian Pausanius (ca. 300 AD) described two versions of the Narcissus allegory. In the first version, which has been dropped, Narcissus had a sister who was identical in appearance and who died. His search for her ended in the reflection of her face, not his, in the pool. This throws an entirely different light on the word narcissistic. The female component has been dropped, perhaps because incest between siblings is deeply repressed. The male–female imbalance has swung from the original Neolithic Goddess (4000 BC) without a spouse, to Adam giving birth to Eve, which effeminated men and defeminated women. The subsequent Holy Trinity was entirely male, but has been counterbalanced to some extent by the veneration of the Virgin.

Today, feminism should evolve not in the form of phallic women, but as women in their own right. Symbols for their role have been suggested, such as feminine principal, matrix, anima, but these lack specificity. The more trenchant name "Kunta" is a proud Old Norse name, which liberates us from the debased epithet "cunt" and from the associated pudenda (*pudor* = shame), foreshadowed by Eden's Tree of Knowledge.

Phallus and Kunta can now engage with each other on the level, and we can, thereby, consider a multitude of dualities, which had previously not been seen clearly because of the prevailing linear thinking, or, at any rate, asymmetry, producing widespread imbalance and pseudo-unresolved, or quasi-resolved dyads. The womb power of the Kunta presents us with the womb's inherent function of containment by structure, adding perspective and parameters to an otherwise unbridled, competitive phallocentricity, rocketing to Mars.

There are many examples of more obviously unresolved and split dyads, ambiguous because the bipolarity has not been adequately signposted, so that the continuum of the third dimension of dialogue cannot occur, as in the case of Kunta, before it had been named. By establishing more clearly defined antonyms, for instance the Phallo–Kuntic dimension (which is in common to both men and women), we can proceed with greater confidence to the practice of dialogue, towards establishing meaning.

I should like to interpolate here the simple dualistic suggestion of Windelbrand to the effect that it is for science to determine facts and for philosophy to determine values. The theme of dualism runs like a red thread throughout metaphysics, and metaphysics could be seen as a form of therapy—the mind's attempt to disclose reality, to negotiate the splits and conflicts. As examples, consider the dyads of the sensible and the intelligible, *esse versus ens*, *eidos versus ousia*, the actual and the possible, all regarded as mutually independent "substances". Descartes did, in fact, go so far as to mention "dual interaction", the nearest he got to the term dialogue.

For Kant, the problem was of the duality between noumena and phenomena, between what is and what appears, and how to find a way of mediating these two worlds. Descartes saw body and mind as split between two "substances" and, therefore, incompatible. Heidegger considered that philosophy should establish inner independence from the natural sciences (he surely is the therapist's philosopher). On the whole, the dialectic of Hegel (thesis, antithesis, and synthesis) is treated as a method or doctrine rather than as an authentic philosophy, and application of this method may be seen today in dialogue as the major feature in therapy. Lacan framed what he termed the real and imaginary orders as a duality, while the symbolic world he characterised as triadic. He writes about dialogue that:

> . . . the omnipresence of human discourse will perhaps one day be embraced under the open sky of an omnicommunication of its text. This is not to say that human discourse will be any more harmonious than now. But this is the field that our experience polarizes in a relation that is only apparently two-way, for any positioning of its structure in merely dual terms is as inadequate to it in theory as is ruinous for its technique. (Lacan, quoted in Miller, 1993, p. 76)

The evident solution to the dualistic quandary is the practice of the "supreme art" of dialogue (cf. Plato), a third dimension.

Content

To establish mediation between the dualities described requires a third dimension, that of talking. But people often do not believe in talking. I once had the pleasure of addressing a group of sixty-eight bankers from South America at Bretton Woods, the birthplace of the International Monetary Fund. I was given the brief of introducing them to the idea of talking to each other in one session, and arranged for them to sit in a circle. The duality with which they were struggling, it transpired, was that of numeracy *vs.* words.

They entered a free-floating discussion, at the end of which the question was asked, "What is the point of talking?" I countered by asking, "What is the point of breathing?" (In this respect, it is interesting to note that the dispensers of aid of one dollar expect a return of thirteen.) There seemed to be a conflict between using words as a way of conveying information through talking and of manipulating people through numbers.

Content and dialogue are the third dimensions when the triple or triad comes into play. While duality is treated by euphemisms such as Russell's "double aspect theory", or "neutral monism", the triad of mediation between the antinomies of duality has met with even greater misgiving: for example, neither the *Oxford Companion to Philosophy* nor the *Companion to the Mind* make any reference to anything triadic, not even the Trinity. The median group is essentially a dialogue situation.

Through dialogue, we enter the symbolic world, which the mind can grope and grapple with, as distinct from the physically traumatic experiences of the material, linear dimension, where painful experiences of the innate mind, in the form of memories, are pushed out of consciousness (knowing with others) back into the body, producing bodily pain, for example, irritable bowel or cystitis, as distinct from the suffering of the mind.

After sixty years of applying dialogue as therapy, the significance of mind has become ever increasingly and strikingly more clear to me. The word "mind" is derived from the Norse word *myndig*, or vote. The meaning of the word "sin" (from Aramaic, the language Christ spoke) is failing to focus the mind. To this day, in archery "sin" is still a term for missing the target. If dialogue is the Supreme Art (Plato) then the exercising of the mind itself is primary. Moreover, the mind as erotic (as opposed to sexual) must above all be cultivated if health is to be promoted, and, therefore, is essential to therapy. Interpreting transference simply unblocks dialogue.

The members of the seminar who inspired me to write this article run a weekly Median Group Seminar, which, as we said, is termed *median* since it bridges the dichotomy which universally prevails between small and large groups, between tribal and social, and results in such dilemmas as the incongruous discrepancy between poverty in the midst of plenty, the destruction of nature's wealth by pollution and banking, and a relentless march by phallocratic forces, totally obdurate to widespread and Kuntic protestations. Without this duality, dialogue cannot proceed.

Another significant duality that is amenable to negotiation as it becomes clear is that of the Old and New Testament. The Old is family and tribal orientated, while the New recommends giving up family ties in suggesting we love our neighbours. This brings us on to look at relations in a wider sphere, from simple dialogue to discourse.

Metastructure or micro-culture

To date we have, as a species, lost the ability to apply any remotely effective technique, any *modus operandi*, with which to address cultural issues, to the extent that culture implies group mind. We seem to have lost a collective sense of sanity, or perhaps we are focusing on its absence for the first time.

The median group, we suggest, offers a simple method of learning to talk to each other comprehensively, and attempts to humanise society, and to transform frustration and outrage into the energy required to think, not only mechanically and digitally but analogically, not only in numbers but with words, in the same way that the Word humanises the divine.

We are attempting to reclaim the ancient method practised over 60,000 years ago by the hunter-gatherers who paved the way to free-floating discussion in groups (up to thirty people), so as to evolve in such groups micro-cultures of their own, even while they remain small enough for all to participate within a reasonable time (e.g., one and a half hours).

This does not in any way denote that the larger group (the median group) supersedes the one-to-one or small-group situations, but we contend it does add a so far unexplored area of social context, within which these disciplines operate, and which could prepare us for the massified complexities of the politico-social area in a direct, simple, and operational way, by "consciousness raising", learning to talk to each other on the level, and, therefore, to think. We cannot only "feel" our way out of the atom bomb.

The median group approaches psychology from the opposite direction to insights of the individual and family inner world, that is, from a position of outsight, looking at the socio-political context. This denotes a radical and revolutionary change of direction. But there are constant delays to its acceptance. It is time we stopped infantilising and trivialising. In a world about to blow itself up, we wish to promote thinking, as distinct from treating thought as an intellectual defence against expressing aggression!

In applying the median group, we are practising an appropriate, if challenging technique that provides the missing link between small and large groups. Having established psycho- and group therapy, it remains for us to apply socio-therapy, and not simply as an academic theory, but as a tool, as an operational technique to save the world. Why be ashamed of good intentions? Why collapse in the face of derision? Paradoxically, dialogue extricates the centre of Self from massification by a circumference of contextual conformity, where chains of clichés pass as thinking. We do this by meeting together with people similarly disposed, as distinct from being obsessed by the mechanical mouthing of numbers. We choose words to barter with, talking with each other rather than studying linguistic philosophy, eventually exploring the creative centre of the universe as well as the social context. We seek, in addressing both centres of self, and of the cosmos, to focus on principle of meaning, adding a third principle to Freud's two principles, pleasure and reality.

Totalisation

Totalisation is as important as reductive analysis, but faces the opposite direction. The centre of the self (a point so small as to be non-existent) in the middle of its contextual circumference (time and space) gropes towards the timeless and spaceless centre of the universe. In the most ancient of Hindu Vedic writings, it is written that in the beginning there was a state of perfection that became humanised and personalised by humans as God. Therapy, therefore, does not only "shrink" into smaller and smaller circles, but also expands and focuses on the vast context of the social and universal, unravelling and disentangling in a bid for liberation. Therapy is both reductive and totalising. The mind, through a series of meanings, finally ends up at the still point of truth: where metaphysics ends, religion begins. Similarly, where therapy ends, faith begins. Greek philosophical speculations end up in religious belief. Modern man's predicament is that when asked "What is man?", he cannot go further than reply that he was an ape. The enormous help of using the mind to talk about these things is represented in *The Word* entering the world of symbols. In the beginning chapter of St John, *The Word* was God. The Hindus had used exactly the same words, several centuries previously.

But this totalising procedure has first to address the global socio-cultural context within which the median group is ensconced, and, to do so, it has first to have established its own micro-cultural power. If dialogue is the supreme art, the median group is the supreme agent, linking the familo-tribal with the socio-cultural.

Resistance to the median group has been widespread, with the result that the Group-Analytic Society and Institute of Group Analysis continue to play Ludo on a chessboard, that is, training people in small groups, themselves included ("committees"), without recognising that they themselves have become a large group. In the same manner, Freud interpreted the horde as if it were a family writ large.

However, many people have become involved with our Median Group Seminar and my book *Koinonia* (de Maré, Piper, & Thompson, 1991). Valuable work has been achieved, for instance, by Dave Parsons (2000) and Peter Garrett in the prison service. This has proved successful, and certainly more successful than early attempts to introduce small groups, since the latter stirred up the past, while the median group addresses the social present and the future.

The median group confronts us with the greater responsibility towards our global, socio-political surroundings and our often inadequate and faulty macro-cultures, even though this is criticised as being evangelical (Greek for good news). Above all, median groups have the expertise to address these arenas. And this is in no way impracticable—if a median group of twenty met for two years, and if each member launched a further group of twenty at that point; then, after twelve years, some sixty-five million people would be in dialogue. It is hoped that this will render a less bleak millennium, this mediating principle indicating a therapeutic function as distinct from the posing of senseless questions in philosophy. It is, as we have already said, commonplace for psychologists to seek the support of the natural sciences, in their linear thinking, but it is for psychologists to reverse this process by mediating the ordering of matter by mind.

Fairy stories help us sleep, bring peace, and, like philosophy, have healing effects; we do not necessarily believe them. Vedas and the Psalms foster optimism; music, poetry, narrative, and art do the same. Perhaps Logos, cosmic reasoning, goes beyond human meaning and begins to touch upon the truth for which we all hunger, logo therapy.

Conclusion

So, what are the more outstanding contributions to group analysis that I would like to see retained or reclaimed, particularly from my own experiences over sixty years as a therapist?

The first and most relevant would be the continued interest in the median group, theoretical and applied.

The second is the discovery that psychology and religion should be given primacy in their own rights and that they should not have to seek respectability in the natural sciences.

The third is an appreciation that there is a philosophy of therapy that should take precedence, and that this has a framework based on structure, process, content, metastructure, and totalisation, based on five dimensions: linear, dual, triadic, tetradic, and a fifth dimension, which I have found to be appropriate as guidelines in applying the median group technique and in individual therapy.

The fourth contribution is the immensely important distinction that must be made to differentiate between the bodily sexuality of procreation and the psychic, characteristic eroticism of creativity. The former must, by necessity, be rigorously controlled, and the latter should be encouraged to be freely cultivated and given full promiscuous status and is, in fact, an antidepressant to address the Puritan culture, which opposes both the erotic and the sexual.

The fifth consideration is the introduction of a new and key word, Kunta, which is the dual antinomy of Phallus but for women, which establishes the birth of dialogue, and which enables duality to be applied as part of the therapeutic lever and is vital in the addressing of unbridled phallocentricity.

And the final contribution is an appreciation of the significant relationship of hate as the driving power of mind and mental energy. The linear dimension is basically frustrating to the mind, which reflects it via the duality, transforms it via the third dimension of dialogue, and, as a result of this symbolic world of the word, is able to grapple and grope, unravel and disentangle the bodily traumata of the first dimension. Mind can, thereby, address respectable massification (e.g., the duality of leader and led) through the development of counterculture, and in this process generate the microculture of *Koinonia*, or impersonal fellowship, of loving your neighbour. Perhaps the excitement over the third phase of the millennium, which is a Christian notion, is over the challenge as to whether Christianity will survive or not. This total processing depends greatly on the skill and expertise of where to apply the therapeutic lever, which of the five dimensions.

If you cannot convincingly articulate a plot for your life, you are living a broken story. We actively participate in the creation of our stories. If we discern a plot to our lives we are more likely to take our lives and ourselves more seriously. Dialogue creates a form of story-telling and plot, and attempts to clarify the situation, equivalent, therefore, to therapy as distinct from the obscurity, the mystification, the seemingly obfuscation of philosophical texts.

Heulwen Baworowska, Helen Schick, Carole Clifford, Dave Parsons, and I consider that our efforts to convene meetings where we attempt to clarify the book *Koinonia*, and in which the name median group has been introduced, represent the only Median Group Seminar that there is. Our suggestion to the Group-Analytic Society that several of the small group committees meet together, however, has met with no response. There has been a curious resistance gener-ally, in fact, to this radically new development in group techniques, often taking the form of arranging matters in such a manner that members simply fail to attend; it appears that the chief resistance to the median group is not to turn up.

None the less, we join forces with Descartes in establishing through median group dialogue the primacy of the human mind and we battle endlessly against the ever-growing threat of mindlessness and autonoma. Once the concept of mind has been established and exercised, a dialogue for addressing the paralysis of inhibition, depression, oppression, loss of caring and minding is created through the inspiration of meaning, sense, and story. Anything then can happen. Levelling and lateralisation between client and therapist replace the deadening effect of hierarchy.

After sixty years of listening to people several hours a day, at the age of eighty-five, I have reached the conclusion that it is the human mind, derived from the old Norse word *myndig*, meaning your vote, which is central. This is an ancient word, which far precedes theology, philosophy, science, and socio-psychology; in fact, it invented them, and they are secondary. That was the reason why Descartes addressed the mind as the First Philosophy, even though mind, in fact, is that which thinks up philosophy and precedes it in the manner that philos-ophy precedes science. It is significant that minding also means caring.

I have realised how very privileged psychotherapists are in even remotely approaching the human mind, let alone healing it; after all, therapy means treating, and, in my experience, this entails not only knowledge as such, but the elucidation of meaning, which in some ways cannot be analysed since it is a process of totalisation, the opposite of analysis. Therapy as minding thus takes on a new meaning.

The following is a suggested list of some of the potential characteristics of the mind. In the first place, it is an agent for reflecting the linear and is, therefore, a thinking process that is human, personal, and unique. It is space and time orientated and its main feature is to observe both the linear and the total. It is capable of choice and decision-making. It is capable of reductive analysis (psychiatrists are referred to as "shrinks"). It is also capable of totalising, wholeness, wholesome healing; it is also erotic, as distinct from sexual. It is capable of minding and caring and loving. It is emotional, as distinct from sensational, capable of happiness and joy, and experiences suffering as distinct from pain. It faces in two directions: the linear at one pole, and the single-minded universal at the other. It registers meaning and focuses, in the final resort, on the truth. We all hunger for the truth. The part of the mind which is God orientated is generally known as the soul (in the image of God). It is, therefore, sometimes named Seer or Seeker. It is involved with finding the plot, the story, and while not necessarily believing in fairy stories, finds them part of a healing process. It participates in dialogue, thereby creating micro-cultures. We suffer not from lack of individual thoughtfulness, but from the shattering of such intelligence and mindfulness by effete pathological cultures, which have to be side-stepped by discovering alternatives so that our micro-culture is no longer an extension of that culture, but a dualistic reflection.

I think it is difficult to grasp the enormity of the importance of Descartes's dichotomy of mind and body for psychotherapists. It had to become a duality, since things and the reflection of things are entirely different; objectivity and subjectivity can never finalise into intersubjectivity, and, therefore, can only be related by introducing a third dimension, that of dialogue or conversation, which occurs when several minds meet each other on the level, multilaterally. This is the essence of group therapy, the treating culture or the group mind. In the median group, individual and group mind cultivate each other, and I know of no other situation where this can occur, small enough to promote identification with self or individuation and large enough to represent a feeling of the socio-cultural dimension with enough time for all to participate. Under these conditions, the group becomes humanised and the individual socialised. Empirically speaking, so far a membership of seventeen seems to be the optimal number.

The collective unconscious means collective mindlessness, which is what the median group attempts to address, and which could indeed help humanise society in the new millennium. The human mind that invented science in the first place could also uncover the unconscious fantasies and schema, for example, phallocentricity, which so destructively dominate large groups and the whole world.

References

De Maré, P., & Yannitsi, S. (1998). Phallus and kunta. *Group Analysis, 31*(1): 121–123.

De Maré, P., Piper, R., & Thompson, S. (1991). *Koinonia*. London: Kamac.

Descartes, R. (1996). *Discourse on the Method and Meditations on First Philosophy*, D. Weissman (Ed.), E. Haldane & G. Ross (Trans.). New Haven, CT: Yale University Press.

Durkheim, E. (1901). *De la division ou travail social*. Paris: Felix-Alcan. English edition: [*On the*] *Division of Labour in Society*, G. Simpson (Trans.) with an estimation of Durkheim's work. New York: Macmillan, 1933.

Eisler, L. (Ed.) (1933). *The Quotable Bertrand Russell*. Buffalo, NY: Prometheus.

Miller, J. A. (Ed.) (1993). *The Psychoses. The Seminar of Jacques Lacan, Book 3. 1955–1956*. R. Grigg (Trans.). London: Routledge.

Parsons, D. (2000). Dialogue in prison. *Group Analysis, 33*(1): 91–96.

CHAPTER THIRTEEN

The larger group as a meeting of minds: a philosophical understanding*

Patrick de Maré and Roberto Schöllberger

The median group, as a larger group, is discussed in terms of the meeting of minds. Patrick de Maré, after sixty-five years of experience as a therapist, has come to realise that it is the mind that takes precedence over libidinal drives and that should be regarded as a primary entity in its own right; not an epiphenomenon.

In the median group, all members have the opportunity to contribute, since the group is small enough for all to participate within a reasonable time and large enough to be experienced as socio-cultural, as distinct from familio-tribal. Through discussion, the inhibitions of infantile sexuality become lifted; this enables growth to an adult level, not as a sublimation, but as a complete metamorphosis analogous to a caterpillar becoming a butterfly, a total transformation. Not more of the same but a total metamorphosis constituting a totally different "substance", a duality of two distinct categories of body and mind; it was Descartes who first established a philosophy of mind, which he termed the First Philosophy (1996). The median group is a

*Previously published in 2003, in: S. Schneider & H. Weinberg (Eds.), *The Large Group Revisited: The Herd, Primal Horde, Crowds and Masses* (pp. 214–227). London: Jessica Kingsley.

primary face-to-face group, which Charles Cooley (1902) envisaged as "the nursery" of human nature in which dialogue takes on a role similar to free association.

Therapists have the privilege of exploring the mind to an extent that has never been done before, and by actually applying Plato's Supreme Art of Dialogue, having established a third principle to Freud's two, pleasure–unpleasure and reality, that of meaning. The word "mind" is derived from the Old Norse term meaning "vote".

Descartes made an amazing discovery when he recognised the certitude of mind. Mind is where growth occurs. Infantile sexuality grows into the erotic mind of the adult, once it has been de-inhibited. Freed from being identified with things, Descartes concluded that the reflection of things by the mind can never be the same as the thing reflected. This establishes the mind as an individual entity, which is crucial for therapists to take into account as of primary consideration, and also that empirical research, cost-effectiveness, statistics, numeracy, and science are essentially materialistic and secondary and were originally created by the mind. When group analysis first started, it was speculative, hypothetical, and certainly not cost-effective.

Minding entails caring and addresses not the how of things, but the why. The human race is endangered by confusing actual with abstract. An interesting example is the widespread confusion of cash with credit. The term "cash" is derived from the Sanskrit word meaning "precious metal". So, while cash is a concrete commodity, credit is an abstract of means of distribution. The creation of credit (debit and its repayment in cash) causes inflation and poverty in the midst of plenty.

Dualism is distinct from monism, or one-dimensional singularism, which maintains that there is only one fundamental reality and which Russell terms "neutral monism". Dualism maintains that there are two substances, two entities, for example, the sensible *vs.* the intelligible of Plato, the *res extensa* and *res cogitans* of Descartes, the actual and potential of Leibnitz, the noumena and phenomena of Kant.

The monistic approach to the mind, that it is the highest neurophysiological extension of the brain, leads to a sterile, repetitive, mechanistic complexity that is distinct from the notion of antinomic reflexion by the mind, which produces a third dimension of creative dialogue and synthesising. Supporting this suggestion, Eccles (1953) accepts the mind as a genuine non-physical entity, where the problem was how to liaise. In 1954, Penfield accepted as an empirical fact the fundamental duality of mental and physical entities, between living matter and immaterial mind substance.

Freud was primarily concerned with the biology of sexuality. In the *Three Essays* (1905d) he finished with the comment "we know far too little about the biological processes constituting the essence of sexuality to be able to construct from our fragmentary information a theory adequate to the understanding alike of normal and pathological conditions" (p. 243). In *The Future of an Illusion* (Freud 1927e), he wrote, "It would be very nice if there were a God who created the world and there was a benevolent Providence, and if there were a moral order and an after-life . . ." (p. 33), implying that he did not believe this. Rather, he saw myth, religion, and morality as attempts to compensate for unsatisfied desire. For us, the mind is in no way an illusion or false perception, since it is abstract, certainly not a perception.

While mind is immaterial and abstract, it is not a passive reflector like a mirror, but plays an active role in establishing meaning, thinking, caring, choosing, deciding, healing, and vision, aided by freedom in space and time. Like any good hypothesis, it simplifies.

Freud used many terms which could be seen as referring to the mind, for example, psyche, mental life, consciousness, ego, spiritual, psychic apparatus. Consciousness is an organ of the senses ("*Sinnesorgan*"). (See *The Interpretation of Dreams* (1900a).) He makes a distinction between sensations and conscious perceptions. The fact of consciousness is a mental process that actually coincides with mental life to the exclusion of all else (Freud, 1940a[1938]).

In initiating the median group, it became evident that people had been practising all sorts of large groups indiscriminately while the median group itself was emerging in a specific direction of its own. It took some years for the Group Analytic Society to recognise this and to agree to a Median Group section. The term itself, "median", indicated that it is in the middle, between small and large; the term was introduced by de Maré in *Koinonia* in 1991, when dialogue was referred to as distinct from free or group association; this implied that it was meaning that took priority over deterministic libidinal forces. Median groups bridge the gap between familio-tribal and society; large groups that between median group and global.

When the logic of physio-chemical numeration becomes confused with the logos of word and meaning, chaos ensues. It is the function of mind to cultivate their distinction in the form of deduction by science and induction by the mind. It is not only chemistry that facilitates the transmission of impulses across the neuronal synapses, but thinking. The mind is bifocal: multitudinous things and the humanising of social issues on one hand, related to self, and the totalising of a unified wholeness universe of cosmic consciousness with the humanising of the divine other, related to soul.

It is fashionable today for group analysts to stress the importance of empirical research and cost-effectiveness for the survival of group analysis. In fact, funding becomes necessary only in a bankrupt economic system that is itself failing, and this failure has first to be recognised by the understanding generated not by economics, but by thinking. Matter and mind are not mutually exclusive, but each is essential to the other, with the proviso that mind takes the initiative. As we have mentioned, when therapy was first launched, it made history and was not initially political, scientific, or cost-effective. Shakespeare commented that the brain is female to the mind.

It is interesting that it was Anaxagoras (500 BC) who first made reference to the mind (*nous*) as the primary cause of physical change and motion, when everything but mind was limited by nothing, was self-ruling (self-generative), and infinite.

Later, Plato followed this line of thought, believing in the spiritual view of life. Plato and Aristotle battled with each other. They are still regarded as the greatest of all philosophers. Aristotle postulated that it was the senses that constitute the source of all knowledge, that is, knowledge is of bodily origin, while Plato postulated that it was ideas (forms) which were primary. Aristotle regarded the soul as an extension of the body (hylomorphism).

We would prefer to use the term "scientific" as distinct from "empirical" research, which is evidently contradictory, oxymoronic, as are other terms such as "ego instincts", "unconscious mind", "psychic apparatus", "dialectical materialism". There is no discussion, no conversation in the primary process, such as in dreams, which, to that extent, is mindless. Collective unconscious is collective mindlessness. Schopenhauer wrote that we forfeit three-quarters of our minds in order to be like other people. In consumerism, people are free to consume but not to think. In Nazism, thinking is the prerogative of the dictator, in communism, of the proletariat, in economics, of the bankers; for Chomsky, language, for Freud, libido.

Another example of contradiction is that of Wittgenstein, who was to produce a dichotomised Wittgenstein I that was repudiated by Wittgenstein II. In *Tractatus Logico-philosophicus* (1961[1921]) he described his propositions of Logic; in *Philosophical Investigations* (1967[1953]) he dismantled his logic and attributed primacy to human beings.

The radical *res cogitans* of Descartes was the only substance to which Descartes attributed indubitability. By acknowledging this primacy of mind, much of the verbiage of modern-day thinking becomes clearer; instead of identifying with the sheer quantity of information, it becomes unified by the simple reflection by a single mind.

It is in contemplation of the cosmic consciousness of the universe that personal meaning is experienced, rather like the holographic fragments reflecting the whole plate. It is a matter of choice, as distinct from invasion by the repetitive machinery of materialism.

The cultivation of the median group constitutes a major development in revisiting the large group. This development marks a radical opposition, from the concrete familio-tribal approach of Freud to the psychosocial abstraction of the mind.

The introduction of the median group into prisons and the armed forces is proving remarkably successful. In prisons, for instance, small groups have failed, since they merely stir things up by infantilisation.

The median group, in addressing social issues, brings about a welcome relief from tribalism. It is hoped that this unique innovation will act as an incentive for addressing other institutions, such as education and group analysis itself. It is the creative inspiration of ideas that is primary for the survival of group analysis, not money.

Middle-class culture is inherently contradictory. Essentially, the middle class consists of skilled working class, for example, professionals, but in a mindless manner usually identified with capitalists, a viewpoint that is shared in this respect by the working class, who envy the middle class, in favour of their own infantilisation, treating intelligence as "cerebral", mutually disempowering. Revolutionaries are usually from a middle-class background. There is a similar discrepancy between capitalist owners of the means of production being disempowered by financiers, who take concrete possession of the credit system of the abstract means of distribution, presented as if it were a commodity. These are all examples of results of mindlessness and lead to confusion unless the elemental entity of mind can be included. Alas! mind is an abstraction and, therefore, usually disregarded in favour of mechanical, obsessional, counterphobic anality.

The median group is a sort of reflective think-tank, which generates minding, caring, sharing, thinking, choice, and decision-making. It marks a striking development in our revisiting of the large group, initiated by Lionel Kreeger's publication in 1975. We are not concerned with the truth but with meaning. Truth is another aspect of the mind, another category, a different "substance". The mind is a reflecting centre. Mathematicians define "centre" as a point so small as to be non-existent and without dimensions. Between the centre of the mind and its circumference is the circumference of reflection, so there are two circles, the reflection circle and the world circumference. Between the mind and the circumference lie the reflections, which are constituted by substances or categories: a triad of centre, circumference, and reflections, which are categories (Figure 1).

There are as many reflective substances or categories as there are reflected "realities" in the circumference: two categories of self and soul.

Minding, caring, and thoughtfulness are generated by the mind, which, *ipso facto*, creates a natural narcissism that constitutes the basic necessity for living and engenders a sense of meaning. Pausanius

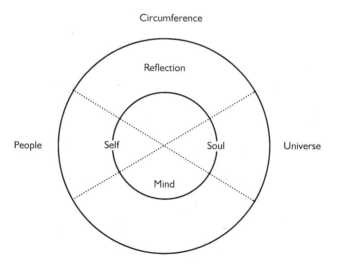

Figure 1.   The triad of centre, circumference, and reflections.

describes how Narcissus had a beautiful sister who reflected his own beauty, which presumably provoked the jealousy or punishment of the gods, so that she mysteriously disappeared and he wandered round the earth seeking for her, eventually locating her in the reflection of her face in a pool and drowning, so that narcissism started as a love for someone else as distinct [from] self-love, in other words, the opposite of what is usually understood by the word, which is treated as reprehensible, causing guilt and shame.

From the beginning, natural, normal, healthy narcissism is given short shrift, is constantly being challenged, implying that self-love is unacceptable, like the little girl reprimanded for standing in front of a mirror declaring how beautiful she was. The net outcome of this attitude is that caring and minding and thoughtfulness cause hubris and Puritanism from all sides. In therapy and the median group, attempts are made to restore this imbalance, so that instead of good things being bad and bad things good, good is good and bad is bad; hanging on to the good reclaims the source of meaning of life, and recognition of what is patently bad becomes openly acknowledged, which is not an automatic process but a deliberate, active determination by the mind. Shakespeare wrote, "Self love, my liege, is not so vile a sin as self-neglecting" (Henry V).

Blackwell (2002) wrote,

This closing down of political space effects a closing down of mental space. The currency of ideas and social discourse becomes increasingly one-dimensional and linear. In education the idea of developing a certain quality and flexibility of thought has become all but lost in a plethora of tests which measure little more than the capacity to give simple answers to trivial questions. (p. 105)

Another quotation is from the Book of Wisdom, written probably about 200 BC and constituting part of the Apocrypha, which is included in the Rheims-Douai version but not in the St James' version. We see wisdom as another term for mind:

Wisdom is a spirit intelligent, holy, unique, manifold, subtle, active incisive, unsullied, lucid, invaluable, benevolent, sharp, irresistible beneficent, loving to man, steadfast, dependable, unperturbed, almighty all-surveying, penetrating all, intelligent, pure and most subtle spirits; for wisdom is quicker to move than any motion; although alone she can do all.

Recapitulation

We have postulated the elemental primacy of the individual personal mind in the process of reflecting and thinking; it is the personal mind alone that singly and actually thinks; everything else, including other people's minds, are reflections of this one and only, unique mind.

From the early beginnings of Greek philosophy there has always been an interest in what, in one guise or another, refers to the mind, but never before have philosophers been in such a privileged position as psychotherapists in engaging in the study of the actual mind itself with the intensive consistency required for treating the mind, which is, indeed, their primary task. The very derivation of the word "mind" is from the Old Norse, meaning "to vote", your personal vote. This conclusion leads one to the unique realisation that therapists have made a profound discovery of a new philosophy that must affect the entire field of philosophy generally.

As we have already pointed out, there have been many indications and references foretelling the praxis of mind. Socrates (through Plato) stated that it was "the mission of philosophers to search into one's self and others". Plato also wrote, "there is one kind of being which is always the same, uncreated and indestructible . . . invisible and imperceptible, and of which contemplation is granted to intelligence only". He also referred to space as the third dimension of space, equivalent for us of the extensive nature of dialogue. There is a duality among the ancient Greeks between those who were primarily scientific, interested in acquiring knowledge and the diversity of facts, in logic and mathematics, and those who were interested in the revelations of religion, the soul, the air, the logos, mysticism. The Pythagorean view was that the empirical philosopher is a slave to his material world, while the mystic is a free creator of his world of beauty.

Many centuries later, it was Edmund Husserl (1901) who, as a good Cartesian, reiterated Descartes's maxim (the *"cogito ergo sum"* of *res cogitas*) in the comment that there is one thing that is indubitably certain, and that is our own conscious awareness. Therefore, if we want to build our knowledge of reality on rock-solid foundations, that is the place to start. He held that the mind and nothing else has a directedness towards something outside itself, similar to Descartes's reflection, and related to Husserl's intentionality, a "wunderbar phenomenon", the world of appearances, similar to the reflections of

Descartes. Reflection precedes the reflected. This is a crucial issue for establishing an authentic philosophy of psychotherapy.

Husserl put it that to hammer his subject–object model, he had to have a hammer. The reflection is a primary, single centre to a secondary, multitudinous array of things reflected, the reflected circumference. It is the mind of reflectioning that psychotherapists address, which constitutes therapy, the source of all thinking. The machine, for instance, computes, but can never think, since it is already programmed, is already a repetition, like obsessions, more of the same, while the living mind is ever new. Exercising the mind is the alternative to this mechanical repetitiveness and, therefore, has a healing quality, but has, like *Dasein*, to be discovered.

From a rather different stance, Karl Marx, in the opening passages of *Capital* (1976), points out the striking dualities of stomach and imagination, the hunger of body and the appetite of mind, of consumption and production, of use value and exchange value, of actual things and their reflections, content and form, and introduces the third dimension:

> both are therefore equal to a third thing which in itself is neither one nor the other. Each of them so far as it is exchange value must be reducible to this third thing. But clearly the exchange relation of commodities is characterised precisely by its abstraction from their use values. (p. 127)

Money is human labour in abstract. Marx did not regard his work as scientific or economic, but "my writings are an artistic whole". The confusion that classical economists make between accumulation and consumption is disastrous. Of his own ill health, Marx wrote that "my sickness always originates in the mind".

Finally, it should be said that the median group offers a stepping-stone towards the greater understanding of larger groups, of which we know very little and which we would hope to explore more in the near future, perhaps by convening several median groups together.

References

Blackwell, D. (2002). The politization of group analysis. *Group Analysis*, 35: 105.

Cooley, C. (1902). *Human Nature and the Social Order*. New York: Scribner.

De Maré, P., Piper, R., & Thompson, S. (1991). *Koinonia: From Hate, Through Dialogue, to Culture in the Large Group.* London: Karnac.

Descartes, R. (1996). *Discourse on the Method and Meditations on First Philosophy.* D. Weissman (Ed.), E. Haldane & G. Ross (Trans.). New Haven: CT: Yale University Press.

Eccles, J. C. (1953). *The Neurophysiological Basis of Mind.* Oxford: Clarendon Press.

Freud, S. (1900a). *The Interpretation of Dreams. S.E., 4–5.* London: Hogarth.

Freud, S. (1905d). *Three Essays on the Theory of Sexuality. S.E., 7*: London: Hogarth.

Freud, S. (1927e). *The Future of an Illusion. S.E., 21*: London: Hogarth.

Freud, S. (1940a). *Outline of Psychoanalysis. S.E., 23*: London: Hogarth.

Husserl, E. (1901). *Logical Investigations,* D. Cairn (Trans.). The Hague: Cartesique Meditarious (1960).

Kreeger, L. C. (Ed.) (1975). *The Large Group.* London: Constable.

Marx, K. (1976). *Capital.* E. Mandel (Ed.), B. Fowkes (Trans.). London: Penguin (first published 1867).

Penfield, W. (1950). *The Cerebral Content of Man.* London: Macmillan.

Russell, B. (1946). *History of Western Philosophy.* London: Allen & Unwin.

Wittgenstein, L. (1961). *Tractatus Logico-philosophicus.* London: Routledge & Kegan Paul (first published 1921).

Wittgenstein, L. (1967). *Philosophical Investigations.* Oxford: Basil Blackwell (first published 1953).

Epilogue

Dick Blackwell

I t is a great honour and privilege to be asked to write an epilogue for the writings of one of psychotherapy's great pioneers. Yet, few original and creative thinkers in the psychotherapy world can have been prophets so much without honour in their own countries as Pat de Maré.

His original idea of a large group of fifty to one hundred members, meeting for one and a half hours five times a week, was apparently dismissed by the founder of group analysis, S. H. Foulkes, as "psychotic". It is not clear to what extent Foulkes was being flippant or to what extent he found the idea seriously disturbed or disturbing. Certainly, the idea has fallen largely into disuse, if not disrepute, within the Institute of Group Analysis, as have the many other dimensions of his work. Yet, his thinking remains one of the truly original, radical, and creative seams, not only in group analysis, but in psychotherapy generally.

His vision of a large group meeting with the frequency and regularity of individual psychoanalysis, and analysing itself with the same rigour and the same attention to small detail, was an extraordinary thought. Whether or not it could be put into practice in exactly the form envisaged is ultimately far less important than the arena of thinking it opens up about the possibilities of the large group. From this perspective, it is first of all possible to see how trivially the large group has routinely been treated compared to the small group or individual psychoanalytic situation. One can then begin to explore that trivialisation as a defence against the anxieties raised by the large group.

Traditionally, the large group is supposed to raise "psychotic" anxieties concerned with merging and loss of identity or fragmentation and disintegration. But exploration from Patrick de Maré's perspective reveals that while such anxieties might indeed be at work, there are equally powerful and profound political anxieties. They begin with the fear of the "mob", no longer under the control of clear social hierarchies and structures. But behind this fear we find deeper anxieties about the possibilities of dialogue and thought transcending the established knowledge and received wisdom and subjecting it to searching critique. It is not the psychotic anxiety of the masses that has to be defended against, but the Oedipal guilt of those in power.

The large group necessarily releases a multiplicity of perspectives in which it is difficult, if not impossible, for any single view to claim a monopoly on correctness, accuracy, or truth. No one single version of what is going on can be the "right" one. It becomes far more difficult for one person, such as a group conductor, or a small collection of people, such as the staff in a therapeutic community, or a group psychotherapy or group relations training course, or managers and commissars within organisations and political movements, to adopt a parental role interpreting and explaining the world to the children.

Patrick de Maré's emphasis on the pursuit of *dialogue* as a lateral, affiliative, and non- hierarchical mode of communication and generation of *ideas* compounds the problem for those who wish to maintain positions of power and status within systems of domination–subordination based on discourses of "knowledge" and "science", which are, of course, always forms of ideology in disguise. Dialogue in the large group undermines the distinction between the teachers and the taught, the interpreters and those who are to be interpreted, the rulers and the ruled. Within this discourse, the prevailing forms of knowledge and received wisdom are not just reduced to one version of reality among many others, but their implicit ideology is also revealed along with their function in maintaining particular distinctions between the knowledgeable and the ignorant, the teachers and the taught, the leaders and the led, and the rulers and the ruled. It is for this reason that so many large groups become playgrounds for word games, verbal sparring and gnomic utterances: anything to fend off the dangers of dialogue and thinking.

Some thirty years ago, my friend Paul and I first encountered Patrick de Maré in the introductory course at the Institute of Group Analysis. Fascinated by his ideas, we joined his first weekly large group the following year. I had the good fortune to be able to stay in that group for five years as we struggled both to learn how to develop a creative dialogue and to gather and retain a large enough number of people to actually have a large, or even a median, group. Paul, whose undergraduate studies in philosophy enabled him to tune in more readily than most to Patrick de Maré's line of thought, moved out of London after a year, so had to leave the group. But, twenty years later, as a town councillor and chair of the housing committee in a Midlands town, he introduced meetings between residents and housing department staff in a large group. It was the first real dialogue between those who lived in council houses and those who managed them. When I reported this to Patrick de Maré he was unsurprised, saying he often heard of his ideas being implemented in a variety of unexpected settings.

This picture of an idea (dialogue in the large group) repressed by the psychotherapy community but re-emerging in the world of politics is indicative of the nature of all of Patrick de Maré's work. He has never been just a psychotherapist, and his ideas have never been just about psychotherapy. He has been, as he has described himself, a practising philosopher, always struggling with the wider social and political issues, and not merely applying psychotherapy to the discourses of culture, politics, and philosophy, but recognising how those discourses could influence and indeed permeate psychotherapy.

Foulkes always understood that the group analysis he invented had wider social implications. But his writing lends itself to being read as a purely clinical text; a model for doing group psychotherapy, for curing the deviant or disturbed individual even if the disturbance is located within a social network. Patrick de Maré cannot be read in that way. You cannot read him to pick up the odd useful idea for doing psychotherapy. He is far more difficult and complex to read; there are no answers, only a particular discourse of thinking and questioning. And what is in question is not how we can do psychotherapy or psychoanalysis better. The questions are much bigger. What is wrong with our whole system of thought; the whole system of western thought, or, at least, the dominant system of thought? How can we learn to think differently? How can we create different dialogues, different ideas, different institutions, different politics, how, in short, can we humanise society?

Patrick de Maré began with small groups, then moved his focus to large groups as a profoundly different sort of group with radically different potentials and possibilities. Then he developed his work on the median group as a specific form distinct from the large group. There is no doubt that these changes in size produce significantly different dynamics and create significantly different problems to be addressed. However, it does not necessarily follow that the small group reproduces the family and the large group reproduces the culture or the society. It actually depends on how you look at them. You can find the society in the small group if you are looking for it, and you can find the family in the large group. It is not just the setting (although, obviously, cultural and political dynamics can emerge more complexly and vividly in larger groups), but there is also the question of approach. Is one setting out to socialise the individual or to humanise society, whether in the analytic dyad, the small group, the median group or the large group? One can either pose the question that Foulkes posed regarding the small group, "What is the norm that the members collectively constitute from which they each deviate, and how do they each deviate from it?" or one can ask the sort of questions that are posed by Patrick de Maré, "What is mind, what is freedom?"

I remember Patrick de Maré once saying that he found it difficult to read Melanie Klein because her writing was so rich; you could only read a bit at a time. Much the same could be said of his own work. The startling assertions and connections across boundaries of traditional academic disciplines and across time (frequently taking us back to ancient Greece, to Plato, Aristotle, and even earlier, to the Pre-Socratics, to an era when "ideas" were a different currency from how we engage with them today) can not only surprise but also confuse and even confound the unsuspecting reader. It is a form of writing, and, indeed, of thinking, that demands an engagement from the reader. Not merely a perusal, a scanning, or even a reading in the way one can read most of the psychotherapy literature, which, within a fairly standard format, seeks to transmit information and "ideas" from the writer to the reader, but an immersion in the confused and confusing, contradictory and conflictual struggle to rethink human existence in both its contemporary and historical manifestations.

One of his most profound observations is that the sort of dialogue that we need for genuine democracy is a skill, an art that has to be learnt, and that we cannot learn it from books but only by practising it in groups, large, or, at least, median groups. Similarly, the activity of reading Patrick de Maré and engaging with the problems he grapples with needs also to be learnt.

He leaves us with far more questions than answers. But they are fascinating and vital questions. Important though his work on the median group is, I have always felt he ended up with the median group because it never seemed possible to assemble and maintain over time a really large group. So, we can still only imagine the potential of a group of five hundred, seated in tiered concentric circles, meeting at least weekly over a period of, say, five years. Imagine, if in a group of that size, everyone could have a voice?

ADDENDA

"[Patrick de Maré] ... dreamed that there was a contagious disease that was spreading rapidly where everyone began battering each other. Once battered, each new member joined forces with the others. An antidote was discovered which consisted in calling out 'Love!' which incidentally is the central feature of minding, or Koinonia."

(de Maré & Schöllberger, 2004)

Reference

De Maré, P., & Schöllberger, R. (2004). A case for mind. *Group Analysis*, *37*(3): 339–352.

Autobiography*

Patrick de Maré

I have always felt something of an outsider, being of Swedish parentage in London. My father was a timber merchant, who came to London from Sweden before the First World War with £70 in his pocket to try and find work. We are of Huguenot stock, coming to Sweden in about 1640. My father was without parents from a very young age. He came from a noble background. He was one of eleven children. He turned up in Hampstead when he was about seventeen and found digs there. Within a very short time he was doing pretty well in the timber brokerage business.

I was born in Wandsworth on the outskirts of London. I remember, when I was about two or three, in 1918 or 1919, just at the end of the War, a curious incident. I was standing with my parents, my two older brothers and my older sister. The six of us were going into Harrods, a very expensive store in Knightsbridge. Outside the front entrance, I remember seeing, and feeling very depressed or frightened by, a group of about eight out of work coal-miners singing lustily in the gutter. My family went in and I remember we had lunch. There

---
Written in 1984, unpublished.

was a small orchestra playing in Harrods Restaurant with men in red uniforms. I was horrified by the contrast. I couldn't understand it. At that time I was very aware of social factors. I think children, even infants, are aware of these social features of the world they are living in. London in those days, with its fogs and so on, was a frightening, dirty, and depressing place.

I seem to remember having spent most of my early childhood in the nursery. My sister was very sick with bovine tuberculosis. I was, therefore, very much on my own with the nanny, whom I disliked heartily and who was really pretty cruel. I didn't see much of my parents. In many ways it was a slightly orphaned feeling; although we were well off financially, never hungry or anything like that. We lived in a big house with a lovely big garden. I remember looking out of the window on to the garden when I was about five and thinking to myself, when I grow up I'm never going to be bored, like I was for that moment. My father, on one of his trips to Germany, came back with a lovely present for me, a little accordion. The accordion has been an interest all my life.

The next thing that came along was my being sent to a mini-concentration camp, a boarding school, at nine years old. It was a really ghastly, puritanical place. Fortunately, it amalgamated with another school and I was sent to another place where there was much more freedom and I was really quite happy there. It was a school that had educated people like George Orwell and Evelyn Waugh. After that, for reasons difficult to explain, I was sent to a military boarding school. This was called Wellington, an extraordinarily tough place.

My transition from there to Cambridge was very, very difficult. I found it hard to concentrate and to apply myself to medicine. I just scraped through. Then I went to work at St George's Hospital. As a medical student in London, I lived in a marvellous studio on Fitzroy Street off Tottingham Court Road. It was rather like the Kasbah. It was a wonderful retreat. It had a vital atmosphere with artists and creative people. This is where I came across a rather strange little society called the Society for Creative Psychology in London, with its headquarters at 8 Fitzroy Street. It was a wonderful place. I met people there like Dylan Thomas, Laurence Durrell, Augustus John, and T. S. Eliot. Although it had a wonderful atmosphere it was pretty impoverished. It was a happy time for me. I was playing the accordion a lot. It lasted two years or so and then came the War. The man who ran the Society for Creative Psychology was an orphan, who had been brought up and educated in a monastery. He was a painter called Basil Beaumont. He was an intriguing, charismatic personality, then aged about twenty-seven. The Society conducted many groups meetings in the Regency Room. Payment was, since he was a Buddhist, made in a bowl at the door. The kind of comments that were made in these groups were very similar to the group therapy of today.

I had been living with a black woman who was a lampshade painter at the beginning of the War. We got married in a Catholic Church, although I wasn't at that time a Catholic. At Cambridge, since there was the Spanish War going on, anyone who went into the International Brigade became a hero; but not many in fact went. At that time I was a member of the Communist Party. I was very keen on looking at banking and social credit. My brother and I marched in the streets. It was he who was the leading light in the movement in which the idea was that money should be merely a means of distribution and in no way a commodity. These ideas seemed to me to be very reason-able and proved themselves in a peculiar way during the War, when there was rationing and ration books, which was a form of money. At the beginning of the War, we all had to leave. I was still a medical student. We were evacuated to West Middlesex, where I did my midwifery.

Then I joined the ARP [Air Raid Protection], as a stretcher-bearer. The centre of the ARP was in a convent in Kensington. I spent a year there, throughout the first London blitz. It was twenty-four hours on, twenty-four hours off. I was a medical student at St George's Hospital, but it was intriguing that although I went through the whole blitz as a stretcher-bearer I never got called out, because the bombings were always on my night off. I never actually went out once, through-out the blitz, as a stretcher-bearer! I found the atmosphere of working-class people a very happy one. I became a shop steward in the Union, which was then called the Transport and General Workers Union. It was quite interesting to find that the left-wing tendencies (by then I had become a Communist, I had joined the Party), were not knocked out of me, unlike the medical students who were curiously unaware.

I well remember the rather incredible atmosphere that prevailed at the time. It had a considerable impact on me. My psychoanalytic mentor of the time was Dr Karen Stephen, who was married to Adrian Stephen, the brother of Virginia Woolf. They were members of what was subsequently to become the Bloomsbury set, which played such an influential role in promoting publications related to psychoanalysis generally at the end of the 1930s. All these activities were rudely interrupted by the declaration of War in 1939, while I was still a medical student.

I carried on for a year in the ARP and then qualified and worked in a mental hospital for eleven months. I was then called up and became a medical officer attached to a battle school in the wilds of Dartmoor. After the Dunkirk collapse, the whole British Army practically deserted. British public opinion decided that deserters should not be shot; unlike, in this respect, the German army, where any soldier who wasn't where he was supposed to be was summarily executed. In any case, this expeditionary force was the only army we had. While at the beginning of the war there were five psychiatrists in the army who advised the war office, after Dunkirk, some 400 psychiatrists were created, of which I was one. This was based on the fact that I had half the DPM [Diploma of Psychological Medicine], had spent a year as a Houseman at Shenley Hospital, and had undergone a certain amount of psychoanalysis. I was pulled out of the battle school, where I was a medical officer, and sent to Northfield Hospital, where some twelve of us underwent Army psychiatry training for several months. This was conducted by Major Bion and Major John Rickman. During this time I witnessed the abortive attempt to create a large group technique called the "First Northfield Experiment", which lasted six weeks and collapsed in disarray when Bion and Rickman were posted to the War Office as a result of unfavourable reports.

Subsequently, I was sent over to Europe on D-day plus four. I ran what was known as the 21st Exhaustion Centre throughout the eleven months of the campaign. This entailed treating exhaustion cases known in the previous War as "shell-shock".

At the end of the campaign I was transferred to Northfield hospital, where Michael Foulkes was running the Training Wing. Now that the War was over, it entailed the establishment of treatment mainly by small groups, the first beginnings of Foulkes' group-analytic psychotherapy. The first small group was conducted by Foulkes with eight volunteer soldier patients. All participants, including Foulkes, engaged in this experiment in their off-duty times. I was an observer for some years of this group work. This experiment proved successful and became widely accepted. It constituted the basis of Foulkes' subsequent development of a Group-Analytic Society on his return to civilian life.

This was clearly a very exciting time for all of us who participated in this experiment. It resulted in the beginnings of The Group Analytic Society around 1950, which was made a charity in 1952. Both Foulkes and I had private practices as well as being employed in the NHS [National Health Service]. During the early part of this time I conducted a very small group of referrals from Michael Foulkes. Shortly after that, Malcolm Pines, Robin Skynner, Jim Holmes, Ronald Casson, and myself set up the Group-Analytic Practice at 88 Montague Mansions, which grew fairly rapidly to well over sixty groups a week, with the help of further associated members.

Two members from the Society, Robin Skynner and myself, set up an Introductory Course, which developed into the first Qualifying or Training Course. The subsequent Institute of Group Analysis was a development born out of this Society.

In 1962 I joined the staff at Halliwick Hospital, which was a Hospital operating on community and group lines. There I learned a great deal about community groups from Lionel Kreeger. At this time there was a slow emergence of large group approaches. These approaches were included in the Introductory Course and subsequent Qualifying Course.

In 1972, I published *Perspectives in Group Psychotherapy.* In this book, I suggested that the future of group work is likely to be concerned not only with small and medium sized groups, but also with larger groups, conducted along the lines of small group analytic psychotherapy groups.

In 1975, I set up a large group of private patients, which started off with over forty attendees. This group gradually fell to around about twenty, and continued after my retirement.

In 1984, a supervisory Seminar was set up under the auspices of the Institute of Group Analysis. This seminar was both theoretical and experiential. This group averaged about twenty members. There was an idea emerging of a group that would bridge the large and small group, which I called the median group.

Editors' note

This ends the formal portion of Patrick de Maré's autobiography, which he wrote in 1988. In 2004, when we visited him in London to gather his papers and compile this book, we asked if he would like to extend his autobiography. We were prepared to take notes. He replied that his work was the completion. He played his recorder for us as we sipped tea and sorted through his files. His work that has followed this autobiography is primarily concerned with his development of the median group and the mind. He views the median group as a vehicle for the meeting of minds and evolution of consciousness. It is his ardent belief that "the only answer to mass violence is mass dialogue" (de Maré, 1989). A devoutly religious man, Patrick was for many years a server in his church, which is next to his home in Hampstead, a suburb of London. There he lived until his death with Turid, his lovely and spirited second wife. Patrick de Maré continued to write and publish until his death on 17 February 2008. He is survived by his wife, two daughters, and several grandchildren.

Reference

De Maré, P. (1989). The history of large group phenomena in relation to group analytic psychotherapy: the story of the median group. *Group*, *13*(3&4): 173–179.

The technique of group work*[1]

Basil Beaumont

A s it is stated in the rules for group members, a group shall consist of three or more people co-operating together under the supervision of a group leader, who shall be appointed by the President, the purpose of a group being the solving of individual problems by the technique of group work. The group members promise to observe strict secrecy with regard to the proceedings of the group. Personal information that might be disclosed in the course of group analysis must never be mentioned, and the problems of the members must never be discussed outside the group.

The principal aims of the group are not only the solving of individual problems, but the teaching and the practice of integration, which calls for the co-operation of every member of the group. Integration is the welding of diverse personalities into one whole, while retaining their individual uniqueness. To attain psychological freedom it is essential that the ability to integrate should be achieved through practice, for psychological freedom is the functioning of the

First published in 1935: *The Technique of Group Work: Society for Creative Psychology*. London: Favil Press.

individual as a valid personality in society. The importance of this principle will be realised if we consider the fact that the degree of success or failure of a Government depends upon the degree of understanding and co-operation of its individual members. This is also true with regard to a relationship such as that of husband and wife, for the success or failure of marriage will rest likewise upon the degree of co-operation and understanding that is attained.

In this age of mechanisation and separateness it has become increasingly difficult, in spite of modern means of communication, for people to attain even a measure of integration, owing to the diversity of ideas and professions and the separation of the sexes in childhood. The technique of group work has been introduced as a method by which the rapidly growing tendency towards separateness may be combated and overcome. For integration should not only be practised within the group, but, once achieved, should aid the group members in their co-operation with others who have been unable to benefit by this method.

The technique utilised in the groups for accomplishing this consists in bringing to the surface and studying the individual members' reactions towards each other and the synthesising of diverse attitudes into a constructive whole, which constructive whole will be of greater individual benefit to each member than his own separate attitude.

The first point to gain in a group is the principle of acceptance. To learn to accept each other the members must reveal their often well-concealed antagonisms, the source of which should be carefully traced and viewed with detachment. This will entail a deep study of the members' styles of life, which in its turn will reveal many individual problems. The life style is the mould or pattern in which the individual casts his life, based on his reactions to his environment. In dealing with individual problems, it is necessary that three principles that are of primary importance in individual analysis shall be dealt with and studied.

THE GOAL IN LIFE. It is essential that everyone should have an aim or goal towards which he is orientating his life. Not only should his goal be a distant and perhaps visionary one, but he should have an immediate and practical one, which may be one of the many steps towards the achievement of his ultimate goal.

CO-OPERATION WITH OTHER PEOPLE. It is impossible for man to lead a completely separate life without contacting other people. Complete separation through neurosis leads to isolation and mental suicide.

THE STUDY OF THE SEX-URGE OR LIBIDO. Sex and the whole life-urge or libido in man is one of the great problems that everyone has to deal with, and therefore it is of importance that a synthesis of experience should be gained, which may be put at the disposal of the group.

Many people do not know the meaning of some of the technical words used in connection with psychological work, and in everyday practice these words are often very loosely employed. A few of the principal phrases, with a broad description of their meaning, are thought to be useful.

PSYCHOLOGY is the study of the mind and its behaviour. The conscious mind is the active, waking, surface mind; the subconscious mind is the mind that touches the fringe of consciousness and by which we remember; the unconscious mind stores memories of the past, individual and racial, which have been long forgotten even by the subconscious mind. In particular, it retains the memory of harmful and hurtful experiences which we wish to forget; but these are living realities that will not be repressed. Further, abnormal conduct is a symptom of an unconscious conflict between these buried ideas. Such a conflict is termed a complex. Until these complexes are located and set free, the mentally sick individual will not find peace or health.

COMPENSATION is a measure by which the personality, finding that it is defective in one part, endeavours to balance this defect by stressing and exaggerating some other part.

RESISTANCE is the mechanism set up against any experience that will touch upon a repression and mortify the ego.

INSTINCTS are the raw material of life, such as the basic emotions of fear, sex, anger and the attitude towards the herd. There is also the instinct of self-consciousness by which we reason, feel, and act.

REPRESSION is the forcible concealment, through the action of outside factors, of the instincts that are the raw material of personality.

INHIBITION is similar to repression, but is brought about by the direct action of the conscious mind, generally as a result of fear.

INTROVERSION is the turning of the life force or libido inwards.

EXTROVERSION is the turning of the same force outwards. Both these mechanisms lead to an escape from life.

The LIBIDO is the sexual life-urge, the creative energy of personality.

A FIXATION is a mental state that occurs when an individual refuses to take a step forward in life that normal development demands.

MASOCHISM is a love of self-torture. SADISM is the pleasure derived from inflicting pain upon another. Both these are aspects of a distorted will-to-power.

A NEUROSIS, in medical terminology, means a functional disorder of the nerves. Psychologically it stands for sickness of the soul and mind. A neurotic is one who is mentally, psychically, and often physically sick as a result of repressed emotion.

In a well-run group, every member will be contributing his full share of experience, and the group leader's function will be that of aiding in the co-ordination and synthesising of these experiences. If the group is being really successful, the group leader will have no need to stand out as a dominating force; but it might be a considerable time before a group will arrive at such a free rhythm. At first the group leader will seek to draw out the members and to elucidate their problems, to act as an intermediary between any who have violent antagonisms towards each other, and to check the group from being, on the one hand, hysterical and unbalanced, or, on the other, from being superficial and false.

There are several dangers that will be encountered when endeavouring to run a group. There is the danger of intellectuality. It is very easy for members to escape delving too deeply into their own problems and reactions by embarking upon an intellectual discussion of some problem, such as the value of money. Admiration is another danger. After a while, the group having achieved a measure of integration, it will be found that all the members are inclined to agree far too easily one with another, and thereby lose their individual uniqueness. It often happens, too, that one member of the group, by the very nature of his neurosis, seeks to dominate and hold the whole group's attention fixed upon himself for a much longer time than is necessary; or, conversely, a member may be so reserved that he will hold himself back and be unable to take his full share in the responsibilities that co-operation in group work entails. Members of a group may find themselves becoming bored while the leader is assisting one of them to unravel a deep complex, and this will show that they are again not taking full responsibility and initiative in aiding the solution of the problem.

Group work is not meant to be entertaining or stimulating to the intellect; it is a serious and human method of bringing psychological freedom and adjustment to people who are not able to afford an analyst, or for people who have had analytical treatment and now want to put into practice some of the help received. Group work will be of value in showing a member whether he needs special analytical treatment or not, in giving aid where treatment cannot be afforded, or as a continuation of psychological study after treatment has ceased. It should be clearly understood that all people can benefit from a psychological understanding and freeing of themselves, and that psychology is not only for extreme cases of mental illness, but is a practical measure of benefit to the individual in everyday life.

It will be seen that group work has a social as well as an individual value, and although we have been considering the technique of group work as applied to individual problems based mainly on separateness, there will also be groups called together for specialised work. There will thus be an Artists' Group in which the problems of individual expression and social culture will be studied, and individual artists will be assisted to reach their public by co-operative methods.

There will be groups for parents, where child welfare, birth control, and all problems connected with the upbringing and education of children will be discussed. Indeed, it is possible to utilise the group technique as a basis for the study of all branches of human activity, whether social and political, cultural, or individual.

It is hoped that members of the group, after they have been aided in the solution of their individual problems, and having achieved a degree of integration, will seek to study psychology with a view to becoming, in their turn, group leaders. For this purpose, Group Leaders' Classes are organised by the Society, to which group leaders are invited to come, on application to the President. For the detailed study of various aspects of psychological teaching, lectures are given, designed to cover all aspects of life likely to be dealt with within the groups, so that individual experience can be backed by a certain amount of acquired knowledge. Group leaders are encouraged to undergo a course of psychotherapeutic analysis, so that they may attain a fuller degree of psychological freedom themselves and have a deeper knowledge of psychological technique.

The aim of the Society for Creative Psychology is to construct a network of groups throughout the world, in which the above principles may be carried out; and it is hoped that group leaders, after a certain amount of experience, will, in their turn, institute groups under the parent body in whatever district they might be situated, so that gradually the aims of the Society may permeate the world.

Editors' note

1. Beaumont's article, originally printed in pamphlet form, describes the principles and guidelines of the Society for Creative Psychology, of which Patrick de Maré became a member and to which he attributes his inspiration for and introduction to what was to become his life-long engagement in group work.

INDEX